THE PATCH

THE PATCH

THE BIG ALLOTMENT CHALLENGE

Tessa Evelegh

Photography by Jonathan Buckley

HODDER &
STOUGHTON

First published in Great Britain in 2014 by
Hodder & Stoughton
An Hachette UK company

1

Copyright © Silver River Productions Limited 2014

Photography copyright © Jonathan Buckley 2014.
Additional photography (p.1 middle row left, p.6, p.7, p.8
2nd row centre, p.9 top right, p.9 top right lower, p.9 third
row centre, p.8 second row right, p.8 third row right, p.8 top
right, p.8 second row centre, p.8 bottom left, p.8 bottom
right, p.8 top centre, p.8 third row right, p.8 top left, p.8
second row left, p.8 Third row centre, p.8 bottom row centre,
p.9 top centre, p.9 top left, p.9 third row left, p.9 bottom
right, p.9 second row left, p.9 fourth row right, p.9 second
row centre, p.9 third row right, p.9 bottom left, p.10 left, p.10
right, p.11 left, p.11 right, p.15 left, p.16 second left, p.17
centre, p.16-17, p.17 top, p.22 left, p.35, p.34, p.37 left, p.38
left, p.39 bottom right, p.45 bottom right, p.49, p.56, p.83
top, p.84-5 lower, p.88 top left, p.111, p.137 bottom right,
p.154, p.161 left, p.162 right, p.163 bottom right, p.175 top,
p.175 bottom left, p.178, p.189 top, p.211 top, p.211 bottom
right, p.211 bottom left, p.211 bottom middle) by Michael
Kerr, copyright © Silver River Productions Limited, except
p.57 right, p.115, p.119, p122, p.123, p.129, p.130, p.132,
p.133, p.137 middle, p.238 left, p.139 middle, p.139 right,
p.141 left, p.141 middle, p.147, p.148, p.151, p.152, p.153,
p.165 left, p.168 left, p.170, p.176, p.177 right, p.180 right ©
Shutterstock.

The right of Tessa Evelegh to be identified as the Author of
the Work has been asserted by her in accordance with the
Copyright, Designs and Patents Act 1988.

A CIP catalogue record for this title is available from the
British Library.

Hardback ISBN 978 1 444 78280 6
Ebook ISBN 978 1 444 78279 0

Design by Ashley Western www.ash.gb.com
Typeset in Eames, Cordoba and Avenir

Printed and bound in Germany by Mohn media

Hodder & Stoughton policy is to use papers that are natural,
renewable and recyclable   products and made from wood
grown in sustainable forests. The logging and manufacturing
processes are expected to conform to the environmental
regulations of the country of origin.

Disclaimer: While every effort has been made to ensure
that the content of this book is as technically, botanically,
and culinary accurate and as sound as possible, neither the
author nor the publisher can accept any responsibility or loss
sustained as a result of the use of this material.

Hodder & Stoughton Ltd
338 Euston Road
London NW1 3BH
www.hodder.co.uk

CONTENTS

A WORD FROM FERN

The Patch: The Big Allotment Challenge is the happiest, most engaging programme I think anyone could wish to watch. The moment I first walked into the walled garden that surrounds our competition allotments, I was beguiled. The colour, the scent, the sheer volume and diversity of the plants growing so joyously, couldn't help but make me fall in love with it all.

I have been gardening, pretty haphazardly, since I was a little girl. My mother is an excellent grower. She had me planting pansies and hollyhocks at a very early age and taught me to appreciate the way nature, no matter how you wish to tame her, has a determined way to do her own thing. The best bits of artistic planting are often because a stray heartsease seed wandered in among a throng of marigolds.

On *The Patch*, our nine teams of gardeners worked for 16 long weeks before the competition even started. Their knowledge and research into the fruits, flowers and vegetables they were asked to grow deepened with each passing week. By the time our team of experts arrived, the contestants could hold their own with the deep horticultural questions that were thrown at them. Or not. Although it was a serious competition, there were many moments of fall-about hilarity. Imagine a kind of *Carry On Up The Allotment* and you'll get the picture.

Our allotmenteers kept their humour and shared their wisdom with great generosity. What they managed to grow, make and eat from their abundant crops was astounding.

For my part, I came home and pored over seed catalogues, picking and choosing things I had never grown but had fallen in love with on the show. My entire garden has had a winter overhaul. I've ruthlessly dug out and given away plants I have grown bored of. I am ready for my garden to become *My Patch: My Big Allotment Challenge*. I hope you are too!

I am ready for my garden to become
My Patch: My Big Allotment Challenge.
I hope you are too!

Alex & Ed

The Allotment

Fern

Jonathan

Gary & Pete

Edd and Harshani

Jim

Jo & Avril

Shaun & Liz

Kate & Eleanor

Shirley & Victoria

Fern & Thane

Sally and michelle

Rupert and Dimi

Thane, Jonathan & Jim

INTRODUCTION

Whether you want to grow a single pot of herbs, or you're launching into owning an allotment for the first time, there's nothing like growing something (anything) yourself. Maybe it's the child in us that never ceases to be amazed when an unpromising thimbleful of seed germinates and grows into lush, verdant greenery, and as if that's not enough, goes on to reward us with fabulous flowers or delicious fresh food.

All that nurturing, watching, watering and feeding: there's a huge sense of satisfaction as the garden bursts into life. Secretly, of course, we know it wasn't all down to us and that nature had a lot to do with it. But among the stresses and strains of life, growing your own is wonderfully rewarding. Quite apart from the productivity, there are the rewards and sense of well being associated with spending time outside.

If the notion of devoting every weekend to the allotment and ending up with loads of bolted lettuces has always seemed somewhat daunting, now's the time to bury that idea. This book, which accompanies *The Patch*, is about looking at growing your own in your own way – it doesn't have to mean germinating seed and hours of backbreaking work; you can do as much or as little as you fancy. There's nothing easier than growing herbs in a container outside the kitchen door, yet they bring fabulous flavour to your cooking every day of the year. Or if you crave a houseful of fresh flowers, but baulk at the cost of buying them, what could be easier than sprinkling some cut-and-come-again annual seeds in late spring and waiting for them to bloom? For the cost of a packet of seeds, you'll get loads of flowers that would cost considerably more. It's wonderful to be able to wander down the garden on a summer's evening to cut beautiful flowers. All you need to do is put a few in a vase or jug to bring the outside in, lend the room a seasonal feel and perhaps fill it with perfume.

In GROW, you'll find all the information you need to get started on growing your own; choosing the best place to plant, preparing the soil, feeding, watering and nurturing your crops. There's also an A–Z guide on growing

This book is about getting back to basics, reconnecting with nature.

Week 3

Shirley and Victoria

Week 9

the most popular (mainly easy) fruit, veg, flowers and herbs to help you decide what is best for your site and your needs. Whether you have the time and desire to germinate seed, or you'd prefer to buy a few young plants ready to grow on, this book aims to give you everything you need to be able to cultivate the most popular crops, complete with invaluable advice from the show's horticultural expert, Jim Buttress.

If flowers are what you are after, there is plenty of information on how to grow, when to cut and how to condition your blooms to ensure they last in water. A simple container might be all you need for everyday flowers, but there are times when it's lovely to be able to create more theatrical designs, so in MAKE expert florist Jonathan Moseley shares the professional how-to skills of creating designs for tables, pedestals and wreaths, and also divulges his own inimitable tips on how to add lashings of flair and theatricality.

When it comes to edible crops, the great thing about growing your own is that you can crop when everything is perfectly matured or deliciously sun-ripened. Nobody will need to tell you when that will be. Your eyes will see, your fingers feel and your nose smell. Walk out into the strawberry bed on a hot midsummer's day, and there will be no doubt that they are ready for the picking. In autumn, when the air is filled by that sweet fresh perfume of ripened apples, you may find it difficult to resist sneaking one off the tree. But you may also be frustrated by the abundance. How can you possibly keep up with the harvest as it just keeps on coming? Thane Prince believes that, when faced with plentiful harvests, deep down inside all of us there is a desire to collect, preserve, set aside for harder times. Preserves not only capture the harvest, but also provide intense flavours, adding a piquant point of interest to any dish. Finding and using both new and favourite ingredients in different ways has been a special passion of Thane's all through her years as a professional food writer and recipe tester. It's a passion she shares with us in EAT, with her favourite staple preserves, and her choice of recipes created by the allotmenteers in *The Patch*.

This book is about getting back to basics, reconnecting with nature and your own little bit of the outside and cultivating your own harvests – but doing it your way. It's about growing flowers as crops alongside fruit and veg and it's about delicious recipes for preserving the goodness of the harvest.

SO GO ON, GROW, MAKE, EAT!

Week 12

Week 21

Whether you're already a keen gardener or you just can't wait to get started but don't know where to begin, this is the go-to section for all the basic gardening techniques. Organised loosely into seasons, it takes you through all the stages of growing your own from planning the plot and germinating seeds right through to harvesting the crops and 'putting the garden to bed' at the end of the growing year. So whatever time of the year you want to start, you can flip to the relevant part of this section and get going!

The seasons are intentionally loose because the whims of the weather mean you can never be exactly sure when one will progress into the next. One year, Easter will be veritably balmy and the next icy cold. Some summers are hot and long; others late and wet. Sometimes, just one hot weekend transforms a spring-like garden into one that's burgeoning with early summer life. So be fairly flexible about what you do when; it's more about sensing the right time to move the garden onto the next stage. Having said that, broadly speaking, certain things do happen at particular times of the year, so by arranging them seasonally, this section serves as a reminder as to when you need to be thinking about what. For example, if you don't spend time setting up the battle lines with the slugs and snails early in the year, you may have a bigger battle later on. On the other hand, you won't have to worry about those airborne pests yet, so spare yourself the trouble!

Not everything is hard and fast, though. For example, if you possibly can, it's best to dig in your compost in the autumn. But if you only took over the garden in the spring, or you simply didn't have time to dig over before the frosts took hold, no problem – do it in the spring. If you don't have a greenhouse or it's too late in the year to start germinating seed, no worries – nip down to the garden centre and choose some good strong young plants. They'll get going super speedily and before you know it, you could have a garden of flowers and herbs and salads for the cropping.

ORGANIC GARDENING

A big reason why many people want to grow their own food is because they like to know it (at least some of it) is pesticide - herbicide and chemical fertiliser-free. Organic gardening aims to create a healthy environment in which pests can be kept under control by natural predators, soil can be replenished

with good-quality compost and organic ferti-lisers, and weeds can be kept at bay with good garden practice. These ecological methods might not be quick fixes like their chemical counterparts, but once the balance has been restored and nature is doing a lot of the work for you, you'll find there simply aren't so many problems to deal with. Aiming to be organic is a good start, both for your garden and for the ecology of your neighbourhood, but there are times when even the most dedicated organic gardener reaches for the chemicals, especially where stubborn perennial weeds are concerned. So if you feel defeated by the dandelions, mare's tails or, worse still, Japanese knotweed, do what you have to and don't feel guilty!

LEARN AS YOU GO

Gardening is something of a learn-as-you-go process, so if you're new to it, don't be overambitious. It's better to grow just one or two easy crops successfully than overstretch yourself and be disappointed if they fail. A good place to get started is to use the A–Z section beginning on page 108. The information will help you work out which crops are most worthwhile for you to grow

in the time and space you have available. For example, if you have a small patch, you won't want to grow leeks, which need plenty of space, take a long time to mature and aren't particularly expensive to buy in the shops. Herbs, on the other hand, can be costly (and often go soggy in the fridge before you've had a chance to use them), but are easy to grow in containers, can be picked as you need them, and will flavour your dishes all summer long.

Whatever you grow, gardening can become addictive, and that's because there is always something to learn. You might decide to have a go at a few exotics for fun, such as aubergines, peppers or chillies, or concentrate on getting the most from your space through successional planting. Alternatively, you may become engrossed in the idea of companion planting and how nature works to create balance. One thing's for sure: your garden is unique. It is a certain size, has its own microclimate, its own soil make-up and, most of all, it has you with your passions. Only by working in your garden will you learn what suits you both. Enjoy the journey!

The Allotment

Meet the Expert

JIM BUTTRESS

I feel really honoured to be the Grow Expert for **THE PATCH**. The programme is so genuine about gardening and the way ordinary folks can enjoy their allotments in their own ways, dealing with the problems that the professionals often egg over. **THE PATCH** generally dispels the myth that gardening is just a load of hard work, and reminds us that fun can be had with whatever time and space you have available. A great deal can be grown even in containers. My three favourite easy-to-grow veg — courgettes, runner beans and tomatoes — can all be grown in pots!

Allotments have changed a lot in recent years. People don't grow endless lettuces and 20 feet of runner beans. There's more emphasis on successional planting: little and often, and growing the 'exotics', like aubergines and peppers. People are much more adventurous now. And there's great camaraderie on the allotments. People have barbecues, or set up shops to swap produce and they also sell sundries. Many have notice boards with a holiday calendar, inviting people to help themselves, rather than let the crops go to waste, in return for looking after their plot while they are away.

The programme showed that a pretty allotment just adds to the enjoyment of gardening. I personally think no garden should be without cosmos, which provide continuous colour all summer. Gardens with flowers and vegetables are both productive and pretty! It's an idea with a long tradition. In the nineteenth century, going down to the allotment on a Saturday with a can of something was heaven for the men from the coal and ship-building industries. At the end of the day, they'd bring home the fruit and veg plus a big bunch of dahlias.

I've so enjoyed sharing my lifetime's enthusiasm for gardening. How many people can boast that their hobby has paid them a living? It's all I've ever wanted to do!

MAKING PLANS:

Winter

RIGHT NOW, WHEN DAYS ARE SHORT AND THE WEATHER IS BRUTAL, GETTING OUT INTO THE GARDEN PROBABLY COULDN'T BE FURTHER FROM YOUR MIND. BUT THIS NATURALLY QUIET TIME OUTDOORS OFFERS THE PERFECT WINDOW OF OPPORTUNITY TO PLAN FOR THE BUSY SEASONS AHEAD ... AND, AS WITH ANY JOB, THE BETTER THE PREPARATION, THE BETTER THE END RESULTS. YOU REALLY WILL REAP WHAT YOU SOW.

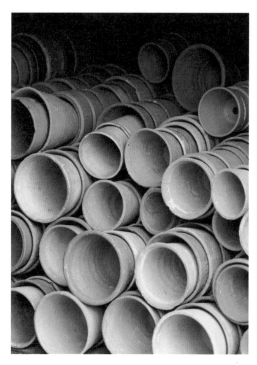

Frost flowers

◁ Even in the dead of winter, the garden never really dies. Robust yellow jasmine flowers start to appear in December and shine through the frosts and snows of winter, providing a warm glow in the icy landscape.

Winter greens

▷ You can enjoy greens early in the year by sowing winter spinach in the autumn. Mulch them well as they grow, then, as the days begin to lengthen, scrape it away to encourage new growth for cropping until the spring greens are ready to harvest.

Feathered friends

◁ Look after birds through the barren winter months. Tempt them into the garden with water, fatballs and seeds. They'll more than pay for their bed and breakfast later by tucking into pests before they have a chance to get at your crops.

Snowdrop secrets

▷ The first of the spring bulbs, snowdrops push through the ice and snow in defiance of freezing temperatures. If you don't have any in your garden, buy and plant them now while they're still 'in the green'.

SHE WHO PLANTS
A GARDEN
PLANTS HAPPINESS

Happy gardener

△ If you need incentive to get on with planning when faced with winter's cold bare earth, hang up a reminder of the pleasures your garden will bring all summer long.

Violet surprise

▷ Pretty little *Iris reticulata* are surprisingly robust, appearing in gardens to cheer bare earth in late winter/early spring.

PLANNING THE PLOT

Growing your own is hugely satisfying, and the great thing is you don't need acres to do it! Even if all you have is a windowsill, patio, or a balcony, there is still plenty you can grow. With a little planning you can achieve a lot – it is all about being clever with the space you have and deciding how much time you have to devote to gardening, along with choosing what you can grow productively, depending on your soil, site and situation (see page 30). Whether you have no more space than a windowsill, or you've just taken on an allotment, here are some simple ideas to get the most out of your space.

WORKING WITH THE SPACE YOU HAVE

If you have a garden but have never embarked on growing your own produce, you can always start out by planting a few crops in selected spots. Perhaps set aside a dedicated corner of the garden, grow some plants in pots or hanging baskets, or nestle a few among ornamental plants in sunny borders. Growing them this way will also have the benefit of adding interest, height and colour to your garden too; for instance, runner beans look wonderful growing up supports or fencing at the back of borders, and in fact when they were first introduced to Europe from the Americas back in the

A whiteboard offers scope for changing your mind while planning. You could also use different-coloured pens to mark up catch crops and intercrops for each section.

Bamboo canes can be used to mark out areas to make it easier to transfer your plans to the ground. They can also serve as clear divisions between crops that look remarkably similar as seedlings.

17th century, this is exactly how they were used – nobody even considered eating them! Equally, raspberry canes and espaliered fruit trees will happily grow against walls or fences and provide an interesting edible backdrop to your border planting.

If you are growing edibles within decorative borders, look for vegetables that are particularly attractive – courgettes have wonderful yellow flowers, and cabbages or lettuces add colour and texture. Rhubarb has huge, dramatic leaves and pretty pink stems that look good positioned at the back, lush purple-veined beetroot leaves make a great addition in the middle, and pretty little radishes can be tucked in at the front, as can the chives with their delightful pink pompom flowers. Finally, of course, cutting flowers can offer great swathes of extra colour to your herbaceous border.

If a sunny patio is all you have, containers are perfect for growing herbs, salads, tomato plants, cucumbers, courgettes, runner beans, chillies, sweet peppers and aubergines. Potatoes can even be grown in dustbins or special potato pots and will produce a decent harvest.

In gardens that are short on floor space but have lots of vertical room, such as balconies, walls or pergolas, hanging baskets can offer useful places to grow smaller crops. They look lovely planted up with herbs outside the kitchen window for fresh flavour all summer long or with strawberry plants that trail fruits and runners unhindered. They are ideal for salads, too, as slugs can't reach the tasty leaves.

If you do decide to set aside part of the garden as a vegetable plot, or you are lucky enough to have an allotment, even with so much space you need to plan carefully to get as abundant a harvest as possible and to make sure you are working as much of the land as you can manage – and not overstretching yourself at the same time.

CHOOSE A SITE

So, the first consideration when growing your own is picking the most suitable spot in your garden. This is down to a few factors: light, shelter and a well-drained soil. Most fruit, vegetables and cutting flowers like a sunny spot, so often a south-facing site is best, away from prevailing winds. Walls and fences will help protect plants from damaging gusts, but make sure they do not cast too much shade over the area. For the same reason, plan carefully if you want to plant a tree or hedge in the same space.

Bear in mind the microclimate of the plot – every garden has pockets that are hotter or colder than others. For example, if the area you've chosen is in a dip, it might be susceptible to frost, which would shorten your growing season, or perhaps it is a real hotspot where Mediterranean crops will thrive but plants such as lettuces might find the heat too much.

Healthy crops start from the roots up (see page 30), so try to choose an area where the soil is naturally well drained, to prevent rotting roots, and that is fairly fertile (although this is less of a worry because you can do a lot to improve its fertility by digging in good-quality compost – see page 102).

MAKE A PLAN

Plan your growing areas so you can easily reach every corner for weeding, pest control and harvesting without stepping on the soil. In practical terms, if you are growing in beds, this means the ideal size is 1.2m (4ft) deep, 1.5m (5ft) wide and as long as you like with 60cm (2ft) paths either side. You might go for long straight rows, or smaller squares, where all the beds are 1.2m (4ft) square or less; or use similar principles to make a more freeform plan with curved beds.

CHOOSE YOUR CROPS

Once you've chosen the best spot in your garden and taken into consideration any less-than-perfect factors that might affect a harvest, then you can start to think about what you might want to grow and where those crops would thrive in your plot. With your shortlist to hand, use the A–Z section (pages 108–183) to work out which crops are best suited to your site. Start with the sun lovers (tomatoes, for example), and give them the sunniest position. Next, choose an edge spot for large-leaved spreaders, such as courgettes, so those space-hungry leaves can drift onto the path and you can reach them for regular harvesting. Pick out corners for long-season crops, such as onions, leeks and potatoes, so they are not dominating useful spaces over the year. Think, too, about what crops you could plant amongst them to get the most out of this space (see Intercropping, page 90).

VEGETABLE PLOT STYLES

The classic allotment garden is wonderfully ordered with regimented areas for each crop. It's still a pleasing style and very workable because it neatly allows for pathways (see above), but there are many other styles that work equally well. Here are some examples.

Crop rotation

Traditionally, vegetable patches are divided into areas for growing different kinds of crops, so that they can be rotated to avoid the build up of pests and diseases and to achieve a balance of nutrients in the soil that meets the different needs of each group. The main groups are roots (potatoes, carrots, parsnips and beetroots); brassicas (cabbages, kale, radishes, swedes and turnips); legumes (peas and beans); the potato family (including tomaotes); and onion family (including garlic and shallots). When deciding what to plant where each year, you should try to follow the best rotation: brassicas follow legumes, onions and roots; legumes, onions and roots follow potatoes, and potatoes follow brassicas.

FREESTYLE

You don't have to stick to one style, you could, for instance, combine elements of a potager layout with those of a classic allotment garden. Loosely based on the quartered principle, each quarter is then further divided up into smaller beds, providing plenty of walkways, with easy access to each crop. Like the potager, it is a pretty mix of flowers, fruit and vegetables, but with the divided-up beds it has all the hallmarks of a classic allotment plot.

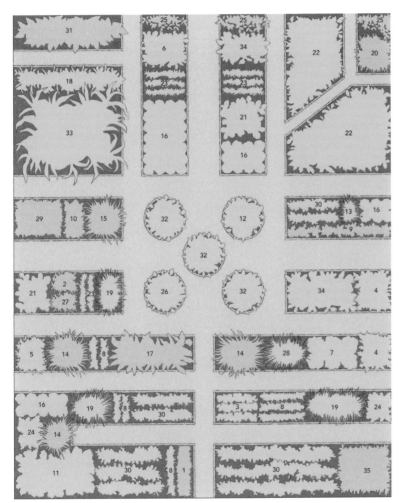

1   Alyssum
2   Amethyst
3   Beetroot
4   Blackcurrant
5   Blueberry
6   Broad Beans
7   Cabbage
8   Carrot
9   Chrysamthemums
10 Cosmos
11 Courgette
12 French Beans
13 Garlic
14 Gladioli
15 Iris
16 Lettuce
17 Lily
18 Mangetout
19 Onions
20 Osteospermum
21 Pak Choi
22 Potatoes
23 Radish
24 Rhubarb
25 Rose
26 Runner Beans
27 Sapphir
28 Shallots
29 Stock
30 Strawberry
31 Sunflower
32 Sweet Pea
33 Sweetcorn
34 Swiss Chard
35 Zinnia

POTAGER STYLE

These pretty traditional French gardens were designed to geometric formal lines with all the produce arranged for visual appeal around large plants as a central focal point. Climbing plants, such as beans, were used to give height, scrambling decoratively over arches and tripods. Each of the quarters can have its own particular style: one being used for fruit, another for salad vegetables, another for flowers and the final one for robust vegetables such as potatoes, runner beans, cauliflowers and courgettes. The quarters are not restricted to food crops, though, they can each feature flowers too.

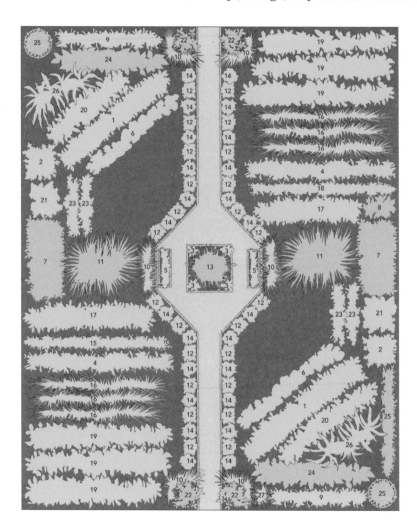

1 Amaranth
2 Blackcurrant
3 Beetroot
4 Broad Beans
5 Carrots
6 Courgette
7 Dahlias
8 Echiops
9 French Beans
10 Garlic
11 Gladioli
12 Herbs
13 Lavender
14 Lettuce
15 Mangetout
16 Onions
17 Orach
18 Peas
19 Potatoes
20 Quinoa
21 Rhubarb
22 Rose
23 Strawberry
24 Sunflower
25 Sweet Pea
26 Sweetcorn
27 Shallots

There's something very pleasing about the ordered rows of crops in a classic allotment – and it's that very orderliness that makes it very efficient: easy to keep tidy and easy for harvesting. This patch has been divided into two halves – one side for vegetables and the other for flowers.

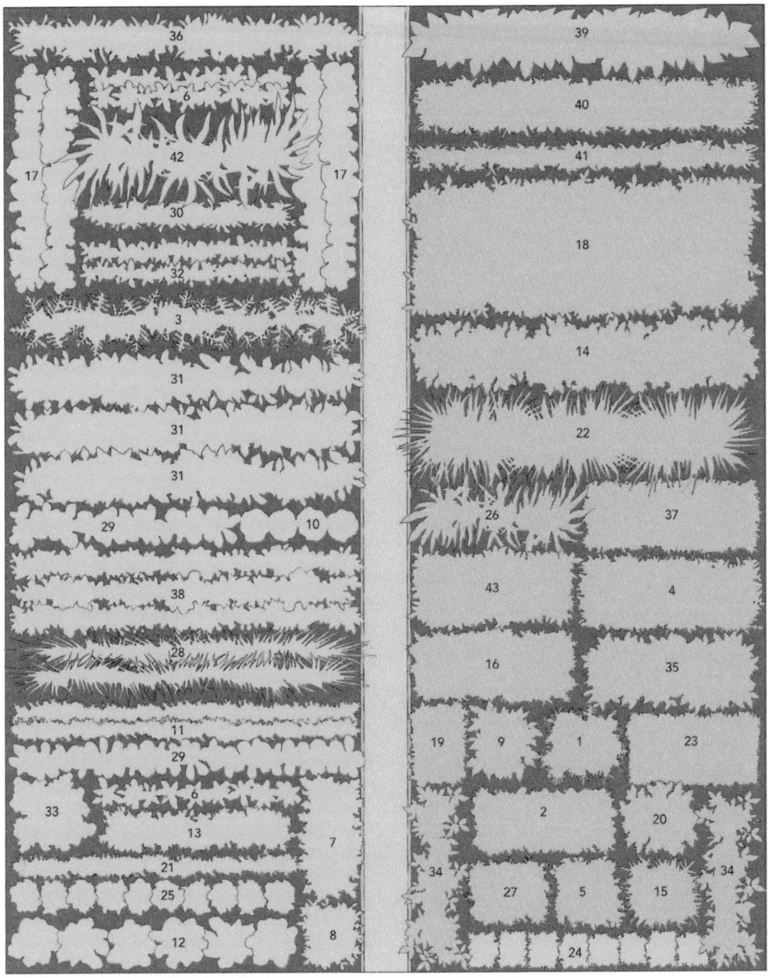

1 Achillea
2 Ammi
3 Artichokes
4 Asters
5 Astrantia
6 Beetroot
7 Blackcurrant
8 Blueberry
9 Borage
10 Cabbage
11 Carrot
12 Cauliflower
13 Celery
14 Chrysamthemums
15 Cornflower
16 Cosmos
17 Courgette
18 Dahlias
19 Didicus
20 Echiops
21 Fennel
22 Gladioli
23 Gypsophilla
24 Herbs
25 Lettuce
26 Lily
27 Nigella
28 Onions
29 Pak Choi
30 Peas
31 Potatoes
32 Radish
33 Rhubarb
34 Rose
35 Rudbeckia
36 Runner Beans
37 Stock
38 Strawberry
39 Sunflower
40 Sweet Pea (bush)
41 Sweet Pea (cordon)
42 Sweetcorn
43 Zinnia

Consider the flowers

If you love to fill your home with cut flowers, growing your own produces an easy crop that makes economic sense, so build this into your plot plan. Quite apart from looking pretty amongst your fruit and veg, they are also beneficial for your harvest, attracting pollinating insects and distracting pests from your crops (see Companion planting, page 28).

COMPANION PLANTING

By positioning particular plants near to each other, you can enlist nature to help out with pest control, pollination and fertilisation. The interactions of plants are incredibly complex and much is still being discovered, but here are the basic principles, along with some useful examples. (The A–Z, pages 108–183, gives information on the best companions for individual plants.)

PLANTS THAT DETER THE PESTS

Strong-smelling plants, such as those from the allium (onion) family, herbs and some flowers can 'mask' the smell of target crops, protecting them from pests. Some even repel insects.

Onions and shallots are good guards for carrots, tomatoes and cabbages, whilst also producing a useful crop.

Tagetes marigolds have an odour that pests really don't like, so they can act as a shield for endless pest-prone crops whilst offering a lively splash of colour to the vegetable patch.

Mint is a useful herb that can deter endless pests. However, it is very invasive and will take over if given half a chance, so should be planted in containers or in pots that can be buried in the ground.

Pests detest the pong of Tagetes marigold. Plant them near your crops and they'll steer clear!

The Three Sisters – sweetcorn, runner beans and squash – make perfect companions to each other. The corn supports the beans, the beans retain nitrogen in the ground and squash retains moisture round everyone's roots!

SACRIFICIAL PLANTS

Since you can't totally eradicate blackfly, whitefly or aphids, offer them something extra tempting on the menu so they'll leave your crops alone. Bolted lettuces can give the slugs plenty to dine on before they get to your crops, nasturtiums make a tasty treat for blackfly, and calendula marigolds both lure aphids off runner beans and attract pollinating insects.

PLANTS THAT ATTRACT THE POLLINATORS

Bees and butterflies love scented flowers (especially blue ones!), which act as a beacon to attract the insects and tempt them to pollinate your crops while they're there! Favourites are lavender, scented roses, purple 'species' foxgloves, cosmos and zinnias.

PLANTS THAT OFFER NUTRIENTS TO OTHER PLANTS

Legumes are able to take nitrogen from the air and store it in nitrogen-fixing nodules in their roots. This gives them a valuable source of nutrients during their lifetime, but this skill outlives them because when they die the nitrogen is returned to the soil to be used by other plants. The best crops for this are: runner beans, peas, sweet peas and lupins.

Calendula marigolds (pot marigolds) attract ladybirds, lacewings and hoverflies, which all like nothing better than an aphid dinner, so plant them near aphid-attracting vegetables.

Plant nasturtiums near crops that are vulnerable to blackfly and also cabbage white butterflies and you'll find they become the pests' top dinner choice, leaving your veg clear of critters!

DISCOVER YOUR SOIL TYPE

Winter is a slow season in the garden or allotment, so it is an excellent time to plan and prepare for the following year and a busy spring of planting. If you're new to your plot, this preparation should start with getting to know your soil. Before you plant anything it is important to determine your soil type and texture (whether it is basically clay, sand, or, if you are lucky, loam) as this will guide you in your decisions about which plants will be happiest and most productive in your plot.

Put simply, soil types range from heavy clay to light sand, but the ideal middle ground that we all aim for is loam – which has an easy-to-work, crumbly texture. If the earth in your garden is waterlogged in winter and hard-baked in summer, you probably have clay. This type of soil will be high in nutrients but it can be compacted – and therefore starves plant roots of oxygen – and difficult to work, particularly in wet conditions. If you have clay soil, for optimum results you will need to aerate and lighten it, to improve its workability. If, on the other hand, your soil is light, free-draining and easy to work, it's probably sandy. Your challenge here will be to bulk it up to prevent nutrients draining away before hungry plant roots can reach them. The best way to lighten clay soil and bulk up sandy soil is to dig it over in the autumn and work in plenty of good-quality humus to gradually change its structure (see Soil improvement, page 100).

A key to understanding which plants are likely to grow best in your garden is to test whether your soil is acid or alkaline (the pH value). If you have (or have inherited) a flower garden stocked with a variety of plants, you shouldn't need to bother with this test because you'll be able to see what is growing happily. However, if you've just taken over a new plot, it's winter so not much is growing, or if at any other time of year newly planted plants just aren't thriving, test the soil's pH value using a kit that you can buy from any good garden centre. Follow the directions to find out if you have the ideal pH balance of 6.5 to 7, below this and acidic, or above it and alkaline. If you have acidic soil you can redress the balance and get it closer to the ideal neutral level by adding lime (see Vegetable gardens, opposite), but an alkaline soil is not so easily corrected. Horticulturalists sometimes add acidifiers to alkaline soil, but in practice this is time consuming and expensive and often over months and years the soil will revert back to its natural pH value anyway. Remember the pH can vary across a large garden, so take samples in a few different areas. The great thing about pots is you can choose your soil.

FLOWER GARDENS

Most plants bought in garden centres will thrive in the average garden, with the exception of acid-loving plants such as rhododendrons, azaleas, heathers and camellias, which need acidic soil. Always check the soil requirements of exotic-looking plants, such as the glorious blue Himalayan poppy (*Meconopsis betonicifolia*), which is one that will only perform in acid soil. If you really

It's well worth getting to know your soil before you choose the crops you'd like to grow – it will help you get the most from your garden.

want to grow acid-loving plants, but you don't have the right conditions, the best solution is to grow them in containers filled with ericaceous compost (see page 40).

If your soil is highly alkaline, take inspiration from alkaline landscapes, such as Britain's well-drained chalkland, Mediterranean hillsides or American prairies. Choose from cornflowers, lavender, rosemary, bay, echinacea, rudbeckia, agapanthus, delphiniums and philadelphus.

VEGETABLE GARDENS

If you are going to be growing predominantly vegetables in your plot, it is important to know that crops prefer a slightly acidic soil, one with a pH value of 6.5. If yours is more acidic than this, don't worry, you can raise the pH value by digging in garden lime. This needs to be done about a month before you plant – any earlier and the rains are likely to wash it away, any later and the lime could damage new roots. Lime works slowly and accumulatively over the years, so don't expect instant results.

ESSENTIAL TOOLS

Garden tools not only need to be robust, but also well designed so they're comfortable in your hands and angled to make the job easier. Stainless steel is popularly used for tools and toolheads as it's strong, slides into the earth easily, keeps its looks and is easy to maintain; carbon steel is the choice of many professionals as the edges stay sharp longer. Toolheads can either be stamped out of sheets of steel, or forged – the latter are stronger, better quality and generally last longer. Always keep tools hung up off the floor to keep their edges sharp and, if they're not stainless steel, to stop them rusting. Sharpen cutting tools regularly, clean off any soil and oil them for protection.

There are some wonderful tools out there for keen and more experienced gardeners, but if you're just getting started, you only need a few essentials.

SPADES AND FORKS

Spades are essential for digging over the soil and excavating holes or trenches for planting. A good spade should be fairly straight from the handle down to the cutting edge, and the top of the blade should be flattened so you can put your foot on it. The handle should be riveted into position. When choosing a spade, lift it to check the weight then test for comfort by pressing down on the handle with your hand as if digging. Spades range in size from large heavy digging spades to the smallest, the border spade.

Forks are used to break up compacted soil and are good for lifting plants because their spaced prongs cause minimal damage to roots. When buying a fork, again check for weight, comfort, and a strong joint between head and handle. If you buy only one fork, buy a digging fork. If you can afford more than one, get a potato, or spading, fork too, which is larger with flatter tines, or a border or lady's fork, which is the lightest.

RAKE

These are used to prepare the ground for sowing or planting out (see page 50), to break up the soil surface and create a fine tilth (so it looks like breadcrumbs). There are two main types: one has solid teeth and is used to prepare seedbeds, level soil or to remove stones from the soil surface. The other is a spring-tine rake, which has longer, finer, more flexible teeth and is drawn across the soil surface lightly to collect leaves, moss or grass clippings. When buying, check that the length of the handle feels comfortable for you.

HOE

These long-handled tools are used mostly for weeding. The Dutch hoe is the most popular; its long handle and angled blade makes it easy to push and pull between plants to uproot weeds and break up clods of soil. You can also use its edge to mark out sowing lines. A swoe, which is sharp on three edges, is also useful for uprooting weeds and is ideal for small areas. When buying, stand it up to see how long it is – the most comfortable length will reach your nose!

Good-quality hand trowels and hand forks that are comfortable to use, plus a pair of sharp secateurs, are essential everyday tools.

A Dutch hoe makes short work of young weeds, but its edge also works brilliantly to create shallow trenches for sowing seeds.

TROWEL/HAND FORK

This little hand spade is essential for container gardening, digging out perennial weeds and planting small plants. Choose one with a deep bowl, which will make quick work of digging out holes and shovelling compost, and another with a narrow blade for working in tight corners. Don't buy trowels with channelled blades or crevices that can trap soil and unwanted spores or weed seeds. The hand fork is invaluable for prising out weeds or lifting smaller plants without disturbing their roots.

SECATEURS

A good pair of secateurs is essential for precise pruning and making clean cuts. There are three basic types: bypass secateurs, which have two sharp blades that pass each other; anvil, which has one blade that works against a flat surface, and ratchet, which you can squeeze and release several times as you cut through thick stems.

BULB PLANTER

These handy tools make quick work of planting out bulbs. A metal cylinder has a handle and markings on the side to show the correct planting depth for your bulb. Twist the planter into the ground up to the appropriate marker, lift out the soil plug, pop in the bulb then cover with the removed soil.

GARDENING GLOVES

A good pair of gloves will protect your hands from stinging nettles, brambles and pesticides or fungicides. The best are close fitting, with a velcro fastening.

SOWING AND GROWING KIT

In the old days, a gardener would get his plants started by sowing seeds into wooden seed trays to germinate, then as the young seedlings grew on, would transfer them into clay pots with more room. Nowadays we are presented with an endless choice of equipment designed to make the germination and growing on of seedlings simpler, more hygienic and more efficient.

SEED TRAYS AND PROPAGATORS

Some modern propylene seed trays have several compartments, which is useful if you are germinating several different plants in one tray. Modular trays take one seedling per cell, which encourages roots to grow down (rather than become entangled with other roots in the tray), so you don't need to prick them out (see page 43) and can pot on without disturbing the roots.

For gardeners who don't have a nice warm spot under cover to get heat-loving seedlings off to a good start, the electric propagator is a brilliant device. It looks like a seed tray but sits on a heated base that keeps the soil at an optimum temperature for the seeds to germinate.

SEED DISPENSERS, DIBBERS AND WIDGERS

Seed dispensers speed up the job of sowing. There are two varieties: one looks like a large syringe but works like a spring-action ballpoint pen; the other follows the theory of the seeders used by commercial growers and looks like a large sponge ball with ballpoint pens on the side. You load the seed into one of the 'ballpoint pens', depending on the size of the seed, fix it to the seeder and deliver the seed by squeezing the ball.

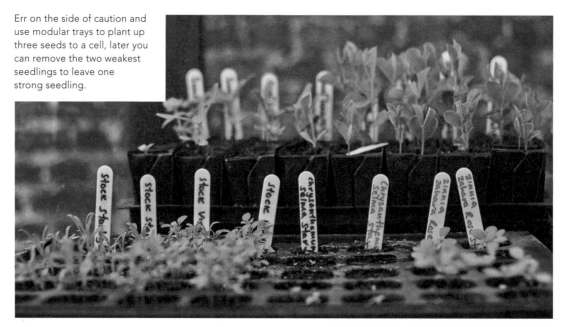

Err on the side of caution and use modular trays to plant up three seeds to a cell, later you can remove the two weakest seedlings to leave one strong seedling.

Dibbers are pointed, pencil-like tools made of wood, plastic or metal, and are used to make a neat hole in the compost for a newly pricked-out seedling. **Widgers** are tapered metal tools that are used in the same way as dibbers.

EASY-GROW SOLUTIONS

Compost pellets are made from neat, compacted compost encased in biodegradable netting. Once watered, they swell to seven times their size and can then be popped into a pot and either sown with a seed or potted up with a seedling. Later, you can pot on the plants or plant out, pellet and all.

If you prefer, you can bypass the whole process of sowing seeds and buy ready-grown seedlings, or 'plug' plants instead. These are an excellent option if you don't have space for sowing, have left it too late to germinate seeds in time for planting, or simply want a few plants of each variety. Plugs can be found seasonally in garden centres or nurseries, or can be bought online from specialist growers – they will be more expensive than seeds, but are still considerably cheaper than grown-on plants from the garden centre. These seedlings must be potted up immediately on delivery and grown on as you would any seedling, or planted straight out, depending on the plant.

GROWING-ON POTS

Young seedlings can either be transferred to small plastic pots to grow on, or into biodegradable pots (sometimes called fibre pots). The latter can be dug straight into the ground when the seedling is ready to be planted outside, and the roots will grow through the pot, which gradually biodegrades in the soil. Good for the environment, they're also good for the young plant, as there's less chance of root damage during transplanting.

Some trays are divided into thirds so you can sow fewer seeds of more varieties in just one big tray. This is useful if you have a small space for growing or want to make successional sowings every few weeks to avoid gluts.

ROOTS AND SHOOTS:

Early Spring

BY THE END OF MARCH WE MIGHT BE BLESSED WITH SOME SUNNY DAYS, AND SOMETIMES APRIL CAN EVEN FEEL LIKE THE BEGINNING OF SUMMER. BUT DON'T BE DECEIVED THAT WARMER WEATHER IS FINALLY ON ITS WAY – BEWARE OF LATE FROSTS IN SPRING. IT'S AS WELL TO HEED THE ANCIENT ENGLISH SAYING: 'CAST NOT A CLOUT TIL MAY IS OUT' – TRANSLATED AS: DON'T DISPENSE WITH COATS UNTIL THE SPRING BLOSSOM [HAWTHORN] IS OUT, WHICH IS USUALLY IN MAY. SO EARLY SPRING IS BEST SPENT SOWING AND PLANTING UNDER COVER, AND PREPARING THE SOIL OUTSIDE READY FOR THE TRUE SPRING AND SUMMER SEASONS.

Slow lane

◁ Some seeds take their time to germinate, so don't worry if some varieties are ready to pot on before others have even shown a shoot. By bringing them on in the greenhouse, they'll all be ready to harden off and plant out as soon as possible.

Provide support

▷ Peas like to get their tendrils onto some kind of support as soon as they can. Pea sticks (coppiced hazel) are an excellent choice as the knobbly, twiggy surface gives the seedlings plenty to cling on to.

Go solo

▽ Seedlings cultivated one to a cell grow strong root systems that are not entangled with others, so there's no pricking out and they can be potted on into bigger pots in spring without disturbing their delicate roots.

Moving on

▽ Once the last frost has passed and the temperature finally begins to rise, it's time to harden off young seedlings ready to be planted out into open ground.

Welcome blossom

▽ Delicate blossoms bursting from winter-bare branches signal that spring is really here. But while they look fragile, they are very hardy and it will be several weeks before the soil will be warm enough for the crops to be planted out in the ground.

Straight carrots

△ If you want your carrots straight and narrow, plant the seedlings into plastic pipes filled with fine sandy soil. Cut the pipes generously long – if the root reaches the garden soil at the bottom, the tip might discolour, or worse still, bend!

POTTING COMPOST

Give your seeds, seedlings, young plants and container plants a strong start by using potting compost. This has been formulated under sterile conditions to deliver a disease-free, weed-free, nutrient-rich medium in which to germinate seed and grow on plants.

The original compost 'recipes' were developed by the John Innes Horticultural Institute in the 1930s to create the optimum sterilised mixture of topsoil, peat, loam, coarse sand, ground chalk and nutrients in which plants at various stages of their development could grow and thrive. These were developed under laboratory conditions and their formulations are still the horticultural standard used by many different commercial brands, and will be labelled as such. Nowadays loam is quite often in short supply and the use of peat is frowned upon environmentally, so substitutes are often used in many products. These have been developed and improved over the years and offer an equally nutritious alternative. Mixes using these substitutes will usually be clearly labelled.

If you're new to gardening, the pile of different composts that greet you in the garden centre might be rather overwhelming. So which one should you choose?

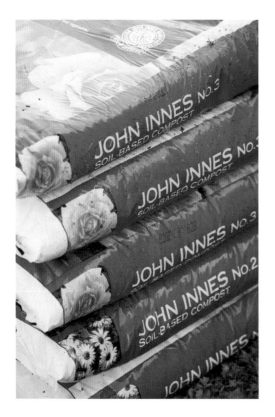

John Innes seed compost
This is a fine compost that contains the perfect nutrients for the early development of plants and can be used in seed trays and seedbeds.

John Innes potting compost No1
This has been developed as the ideal blend for potting on seedlings, containing a base mix of fertilisers.

John Innes compost No2
With double the base mix and therefore nutrients of No1, this compost was developed to meet the needs of young plants as they develop from seedlings and should be used when potting on.

John Innes compost No3
No3 contains the highest amount of base mix and is intended for hungry pot plants and long-term container plants.

John Innes ericaceous compost
This lime-free compost has been developed for acid-loving plants such as azaleas, camellias, heathers, magnolias and rhododendrons.

PEAT-BASED OR PEAT-FREE?

For decades, composts had used peat as their base blend. The cost to the environment of using this natural compost as a growing medium is that we have lost 94 per cent of our lowland peatbogs, in the process driving global warming and destroying valuable natural habitats for innumerable animals, birds and plants. In response to this environmental crisis, many of the major compost manufacturers now use peat-free alternatives by substituting peat for coir (made from coconut husks), shredded bark and green compost. Whenever possible, try to buy peat-free, but when using these composts, check how the compost will affect the watering and feeding requirements, as these will differ depending on their particular constituents.

MULTIPURPOSE COMPOSTS

These are generally less expensive to buy than specific-use composts and their blend of nutrients will support plants in many different conditions and stages of growth, from seed germination to seedlings, and long-term plantings in containers.

CONTAINER COMPOSTS

The best of these include slow-release feed and water-retaining granules. They should provide enough food to support the plants in the container for up to two months, after which you'll need to add more nutrients.

GROW BAGS

These are handily sized – and shaped – inexpensive bags of compost in which you can grow vegetables such as tomatoes and runner beans throughout the season. They generally contain less added nutrients than multipurpose compost and are intended to be topped up with feed over the growing period.

BULB FIBRE

Flower bulbs are the plant's own food store, lying dormant in the ground until the soil warms up and the plant begins to grow. For this reason, bulbs don't need the extra feed added to commercial compost and can be planted straight into untreated ground. If you're planting indoors, use bulb fibre, which has oyster shell and charcoal added for drainage to keep the bulbs from rotting and to keep them smelling sweet.

Potting compost and watering

Never let potting compost dry out as it can be very difficult to re-wet. Although some compost mixes contain water-retaining gel, it's always a good idea to add more of this when potting up containers because they can dry out very quickly during hot spells. If compost does dry out, submerge the whole container in a bucket of water until it has become thoroughly re-wetted. The water tends to run off dried-out compost so you will need to water then re-water several times over a period of an hour or so.

STARTING OFF SEEDLINGS

Early spring weather is volatile. Extending from late February until the end of April, spring can be windy, frosty and even snowy, or there might be warm, balmy days. Now is the time to get seedlings going, but frost-bitten young plants will set you back to square one. The safest solution to this problem, if you want to germinate your own seeds, is to start them off in the greenhouse (if you have one) or in a light spot indoors, then harden them off outside as the weather warms up (see page 44).

SEEDS OR PLUGS?

Starting plants off under cover gives you choices. Germinating from seed is the most economical way to raise plants, or you can try the more costly alternative of buying plug plants, which are small seedlings that are ready to pot on. Although expensive, plugs are less work, possibly more reliable, and incur less wastage, as you only bring on as many plants as you need or want.

GERMINATING SEEDS

Commercial seeds are treated so that they offer the best possible germination results, but that success is also dependent on giving them the best possible chance to do so. All seeds are dormant until the conditions are right for them to germinate – the levels of water, light and temperature must be just so. Most seeds need a minimum temperature of 18°C (65°F) to germinate, though different seeds have different requirements and these

Modular seed boxes make it easy to raise a few seedlings of many different varieties, which means you can avoid gluts and keep up with the harvest.

Skip pricking out by sowing seeds in modular seedboxes (left). Smaller seeds can be sown into seedboxes and then pricked out into rows once they are big enough to handle (right).

are explained on their packaging. Essentially, some seeds might need to be soaked before planting; others can simply be sown into warm, watered compost. Large seeds, such as sunflowers, beans, peas and courgettes, produce good strong seedlings that can get off to a quick start, but generally the smaller the seed, the smaller the seedlings and the longer they take to get going. Germination rates can vary depending on the time of year. For example, carrots planted in late winter can take 21 days to germinate, whilst those planted in spring take just 14 (see Carrots, page 116).

STARTER'S ORDERS

Large seeds can be started off one to a pot then potted on into larger pots as they grow, but sowing small seeds is much more fiddly. Sprinkle them into seed trays filled with seed compost, then water using the delicate rose attachment on your watering can to avoid displacing them. Place the watered trays in a light position away from direct sunlight, which could scorch the tiny seedlings. Put labels into each tray, recording the name and date of sowing, particularly if you have numerous trays or many varieties sown into one tray. Once the seeds have germinated, the seedlings should grow fairly rapidly and will become densely packed. When they are strong enough, they must be thinned out (or 'pricked out') to give them space to grow and thrive.

PRICKING OUT

You can prick out the seeds either into seed trays, which can take about 50 seedlings, or small pots. Fill the trays with good-quality seed compost, then prepare five lines of ten holes: one for each seedling. Gently hold one of the seedlings by a leaf (NOT the stem) and carefully separate its roots using a dibber. Lower the roots into the hole and press the compost firmly around them. Repeat until you've filled the tray. Label the plants, recording the name and date. Water and place in a light position away from direct sunlight. Keep watered until the seedlings are ready to move into larger pots.

HARDENING OFF

Greenhouses or warm windowsills indoors provide the perfect climate-controlled conditions for bringing on seedlings, but there comes a time when young plants must grow up and venture into the outside world. But the change in environment can be a shock to tender young things, so first they need to be acclimatised to the cooler temperatures outdoors, a process called 'hardening off'. This typically takes two to three weeks, during which time the leaf structure thickens and becomes more waxy, making the plant more resilient and better able to withstand spring's changeable weather.

START SLOWLY

Start to harden off the plants once the risk of frost is over. During the first week, put the plants outdoors against a south-facing wall on a warm but overcast day and bring them indoors overnight. If you have a cold frame, they can be left in this overnight with the lid (known as the light) shut.

By the second week plants can be left out on colder days with the protection of a layer of horticultural fleece or a cloche, but they still need to be brought in at night. In the third week the plants can be left uncovered during the day and covered with a fleece or cloche at night. By the end of that week the plants should be strong enough to be left uncovered all day and

night. During this whole process, check the plants regularly. If the leaves turn blotchy or they stop growing, slow down the hardening-off process. If there is any damage caused by low temperatures, cut out the damaged growth if the plant is large and strong enough to take it.

After careful hardening off, the plants are ready to be planted out into the ground. However, keep an eye on the weather forecast during this time and be ready to cover the plants with fleece or a cloche if there is a risk of late frost. This is likely to be the state of affairs up until late April or early May in most of the UK, but freak frosts can occur even in June in parts of Scotland.

Protecting from frost
Horticultural fleece (left) is available in sheets and comes in several weights. For larger plants, there are 'jackets', some of which come with zips. Cloches can range from bag-like or pop-up fleeces, which look much like mini pop-up tents, to traditional glass or plastic cloches that fit over individual plants, or polythene 'tunnels' that protect rows of vegetables.

Cloches can be placed over seedlings in their pots or trays when hardening off. You can also put them over bare earth for a few days or weeks to help warm the ground before planting out, or put them over newly planted out crops if there is a chance of a late-night frost.

Cold frames are the perfect choice if you don't have the space, time or budget for a greenhouse. As spring progresses, close the glass lids (lights) to help germinate seedlings. Then, when hardening off, lift the lights during the day and replace them at night to protect the plants against frosts.

GREENHOUSE GROWING

If you're lucky enough to have a greenhouse in your garden or on your allotment, you'll be able to germinate your own seeds and bring on seedlings, safely protected from the frost. You'll also be able to grow some of the more heat-loving plants that might not thrive in a British summer, such as aubergines, peppers, chillies, cucumbers and all types of tomatoes. Having said that, investing in a new greenhouse isn't for gardening beginners. They're expensive to buy, and time-consuming. If you inherit one (perhaps when you buy a new property), you'll need to know how to use it effectively. Here are the basics.

KEEP IT SCRUPULOUSLY CLEAN

You'll need to thoroughly scrub the greenhouse inside and out at least once a year, or, if you've inherited one, before you start using it. There are plenty of nooks and crannies inside that can harbour fungus, bacteria, germs and insects, and if they're not eliminated, these will infest your new seedlings. Outside, you'll need to remove algae, moss and grime that can also harbour nasties and cut out light. Remove all the plants and thoroughly scrub using specialist greenhouse cleaners or domestic cleaning products. Scrape out any dirt trapped between the panes using a scraper or plant label. Do this in the summer when it's safe to put the plants outside or the winter when the greenhouse is empty.

A thermometer is essential to check the greenhouse is warm enough for seeds to germinate. Later in the year, it will alert you if the greenhouse is getting too hot.

In colder climates, tomatoes can only be grown under glass; having a greenhouse in milder climates means you can grow a wider range of varieties.

HEAT CONTROL

There's a wide range of greenhouse heaters available from specialist suppliers. However, for safety reasons, these need to be fitted by a qualified electrician using outdoor cabling. If you have garden lighting, he might be able to take a spur off this. But this is expensive and there are other methods of heat control. In early spring, when you're germinating seed, use an electric heated propagator in the conservatory for the most tender plants.

VENTILATION

Greenhouses need to be properly ventilated to avoid the growth of fungus and mould and to stop the temperature from rising much above 27°C/81°F, at which point plant damage can begin to occur. You can buy vent openers that automatically open and close the vents as the temperature changes. If you don't have electricity in your greenhouse, choose a solar-powered version. Once the weather is warmer, you can leave the door open, as well as any vents or louvres, during the day.

SHADING

In the summer, direct sunlight can scorch young plants, so you need to protect them from searing heat but still allow all-important light to reach them. Here are some strategies to solve this conundrum:

Shading paints can be diluted and painted onto the outside of glass roofs. As the summer progresses and the sun gets stronger, you can paint on more layers. At the end of the summer, wash them off. This is best for glass: it doesn't wash off polycarbonate or acrylic glazing quite so easily.

Shade netting can be fixed with clips to the inside of the roof or, less easily, to the outside.

Special greenhouse blinds, either internal or external, are available and can be fitted by experts. The internal blinds are available in several hi-tech materials designed to deal with different degrees of shading and breathability to help with ventilation.

If you want to germinate seed, get plants started off early in the season or grow exotic tender varieties, you will need a greenhouse.

DAMPING DOWN

In high summer, the humidity in the greenhouse can fall, and plants can wilt. You'll need to damp down, which simply means watering the floor. Do not wet the plants as this can cause fungal growth. The water from the floor will evaporate and the leaves take their moisture from the air. You'll need to do this three times a day in the height of hot summers.

IRRIGATION

Unless you're able to water the plants in your greenhouse every day yourself, you'll need to rig up some kind of irrigation system.

Caplliary matting is the simplest as it holds water that the plants can draw up themselves when they need it. The matting can be cut to any size and used in combination with self-watering trays or reservoirs that hold up to 3 litres (5 pints) of water.

Holiday watering spikes are available either with their own flask, or as attachments to ordinary plastic drinks bottles. They automatically adjust to the weather conditions to deliver water to the roots of your plants. They are not reliable enough as a permanent solution, but could help over holidays.

Gravity-fed dripper systems that come with tubing to deliver water to individual plants and pots are a good non-electrical solution. The system is gravity-fed from a reservoir – the higher you place the reservoir, the faster the water flows.

Automatic watering systems are the very best, though most expensive, solution. They depend on an electrical source, though if you have an automatic irrigation system in your garden, it will not be too difficult to take a spur off it for the greenhouse.

PEST CONTROL

The warm environment and abundance of plant material makes the greenhouse a paradise for pests. You need to do all you can to avoid introducing them from the garden. Only use commercial potting compost that will have been sterilised, and scrub down with disinfectant any tools that have been used

Position the greenhouse in a sheltered position such as near a wall for maximum heat, but make sure it is not overshadowed. Getting the right site is especially important if you don't have heating.

A greenhouse will give you a head start on the growing season; you can be germinating seed and raising seedlings early in the spring which will bring forward your harvest and extend the season.

outside. Do the same with pots and clear up any fallen leaves or petals on the greenhouse floor.

As well as being a welcome sign to garden pests, greenhouses have their own bugs: red spider mite, glasshouse whitefly, leaf hopper mealybugs and scale insects. These can be controlled with chemical insecticides available from garden centres, or choose the biological route by ordering tiny natural predators on the internet. Alternatively, try a neem oil-based spray that inhibits the development of insects damaging the plants.

Glasshouse leafhopper is a tiny sap-sucking insect that causes discoloration of the leaves. The plant will survive and grow new leaves once the creature is eradicated. A tiny parasitic wasp, *Anagrus atomus*, can deal with the problem.

Glasshouse red spider mite also sucks sap, causing leaf damage and leaf drop. You can also sometimes spot some of their tiny webs. It can be hard to get rid of red spider mite because it breeds rapidly in the summer and some mites have developed a resistance to insecticides. A biological solution is *Phytoseiulus persimilis*, which feeds on the eggs of red spider mite.

Glasshouse whitefly is sap-sucking and secretes sticky honeydew, which then encourages the growth of sooty mould. Whitefly are visible to the naked eye and fly up when the plant is disturbed. Use the parasitic wasp *Encarsia formosa* to keep it under control.

Scale insects look like bumps underneath the leaves and on the stems of plants. They are also sap-sucking and weaken the growth of the plants. Control them with the parasitic wasp *Metaphycus helvolus*.

All plants should be thoroughly hardened off before planting out. They need to be strong enough to be left outside all day and overnight for several days while they're still in their pots before they can deal with the next shock of being dug into the more exposed open ground.

The best time to plant out is on a warm, cloudy afternoon, as the plants might get a little droopy if you do this on a sunny day. Ideally, you will have already improved the soil the previous autumn by digging it over and incorporating compost or well-rotted manure (see page 100). This will have broken down over the winter, especially if there have been frosts, releasing the nutrients and helping to aerate the soil. If you didn't manage to do that, depending on which crops you want to grow, dig over the soil and work in some well-rotted compost a few weeks before planting out.

DIBBING

This is the quickest and most efficient way to plant out small seedlings. Prepare the ground by digging it over and removing all the weeds. Thoroughly water the plants in their pots and allow the water to drain

With the combination of longer warmer days and plenty of ground space to spread their roots, once the young plants are planted into the open ground, they really begin to burgeon.

Once the frosts are over and you've hardened off your young plants, they can be planted out into their final positions along with the appropriate supports and protection.

If there's still a chance of frost, cover vulnerable plants with a blanket of horticultural fleece.

through, and while it is doing so, rake the soil to level it and break up any clods of earth. Next, mark out the rows using pegs and garden string at the required spacings, depending on what crop you want to grow. Then take your dibber, which is a small, pointed hand tool, make a hole in the ground, pop in the seedling and press compost around its roots. Mulch around the rows (see page 66) to help keep down the weeds and to retain the moisture in the soil.

THE BIGGER POTS

Plants that are too large to be planted using a dibber need a little more individual attention. Prepare the ground as before and water each pot well. Decide on the positions of the plants, checking the spacing recommended for the species you are planting, then place the pots in position on top of the soil. Use a hand trowel to dig a hole that is generous enough to accommodate the pot and leave a little space all around. Gently tip the plant out of its pot without disturbing the roots then place it in the hole. Pack compost around the root ball and press it in with your fingers, then scatter over a pinch of blood, fish and bone. Finally, water in the plant – this both gives the plant a good start and settles the compost around the roots.

If you want your plants in rows, instead of digging individual holes, use a garden spade to dig a trench deep and wide enough to accommodate the pots with room to spare. Throw some enriched compost or fertiliser in the bottom of the trench, carefully remove the plants from their pots and place them in position, then fill around the plants with enriched compost and press them in the same way as before. Very lightly mulch around them (see page 66) to help keep down the weeds and retain the moisture in the soil.

PLANNING THE WATERING

Watering the garden might not be high on your priority list right now, thanks to April showers, but while the garden is still relatively bare this is a good time to plan ahead and get the right system in place before water supply does become an issue. If plants are to thrive, resist disease and produce an abundant harvest, the garden will need on average about 1.25cm (½in) rainfall or the equivalent in water every week in spring and double that in summer.

CONSERVE THE WATER LEVELS

Waiting until summer, when the moisture levels in the ground are already depleted, then splashing on a bit of water every other day just won't do. For healthy roots and strong plants you need to establish a decent moisture level in the soil now, and aim to maintain that throughout the summer. The soil can be dry to the touch on the surface but it should be damp to a spade's depth down. Digging in plenty of composted material and applying a layer of mulch to the surface of the soil will help retain the moisture levels through the seasons (see Mulch, page 66).

WATERING CANS, HOSES AND WATER BUTTS

Watering cans are useful when potting on, watering in newly planted plants, or for container gardening, but for other jobs they can be very labour intensive. Hoses make the job of watering larger areas much easier, particularly when a good soaking is in order, and come with a variety of clip-on attachments for connecting to the garden tap, spraying, sprinkling and adding on extra hose lengths.

However, since hoses are water guzzlers, in times of drought many local councils impose hosepipe bans just when your plants need water the most. One way around this is to install one or several water butts that can be used to collect water from any roof that has gutters and downpipes by using a downpipe connector kit. Choose a butt with a tap that can be used to connect the hose (the ban only applies when the hose is connected to the mains water supply).

You can also water plants with 'grey water', which is waste household water from baths, basins and washing machines, as most detergents won't affect plants. Do not use toilet water or water that may have traces of bleach or other strong chemicals, such as oven cleaner, in it. Use a watering can or bucket to deliver grey water as you have it – if you store it in a butt, it will soon become foul and smelly.

AUTOMATIC WATERING SYSTEMS

Simple garden irrigation systems are remarkably efficient – they generally use 90 per cent less water than traditional spray guns or lawn sprinklers, and for that reason they are usually exempt from hosepipe bans, but check the restrictions in your local area. The simplest of all to use is a soaker hose, which has a series of tiny holes along its length. Laid in the vegetable patch or flower garden, water is delivered straight to the roots when the tap (which can be controlled by a timer) is turned on.

Micro-irrigation systems are more sophisticated. They're composed of a system of 13mm (½in) pipelines laid around the garden. Micro-tubing connected to the pipelines delivers water to individual beds or plants via various drippers, micro-jets and mini sprinklers. The system is controlled by a timer attached to the garden tap, which allows the garden to be watered (often for less than five minutes at a time) during the hours of darkness when there is no evaporation. Garden centres sell various easy-to-fit kits for particular situations, such as a border of a particular size, a hedge of a particular length, 20 pots, the greenhouse, or even growbags. More complicated systems need to be installed by professional gardeners or irrigation specialists.

As the temperatures rise and the rains give way to dryer days, give the garden a good drink once the sun is going down. The leaves could be scorched if water gets on them whilst the sun is high in the middle of the day.

In spring, before pests with wings have taken to the air and when plant growth is limited to roots and the newest of shoots, it's slugs, snails and soil dwellers (see A–Z entries for particular pests of specific plants) that offer the greatest challenges to establishing seedlings – sometimes devastating them before they even have much of a chance to get off the starting blocks. So spring is the ideal time to arm yourself with the most efficient weapons to keep those pests under control and protect your young plants.

SLUGS AND SNAILS

Slugs are soft-bodied, orange, brown or black molluscs that vary in adult sizes between 5 and 12cm (2 and 5in) long. They are 'nomads' and travel to areas where there are fewer slugs and they can move both under and over ground, causing damage wherever they go. Snails are similar but their shells are their homes and they keep within a limited territory. Snails are limited to above-ground activity, but as their shells can protect them from drying out, they can also move around at all times and cause damage higher up the plants.

Slugs and snails like nothing better than a banquet of new soft growth, especially on lettuces, tulips, sweet peas, spring growth and any seedlings. Slugs also like to tuck into potatoes and root crops. They will do their worst at night, especially during wet weather. Decimated leaves first thing in the

Protect young seedlings from slug damage by planting them in copper collars. The copper will give the slugs an unwelcome electric shock!

morning bear witness to their after-hours activities. If you haven't already taken action, waste no time; slugs reproduce in spring, so you need to reduce their numbers before they do so. Each slug lays up to 500 translucent eggs about 3mm across on the underside of low leaves, in compost heaps and in the soil in spring, so destroy any you see. If you finely till seedbeds you will expose these eggs which will then dry out in the sun or be eaten by other creatures.

Slugs don't like slithering over moisture-absorbent materials, so create barriers to help protect your plants. You can buy organic barrier methods to sprinkle around the plants, or you can use broken-up eggshells, wood ash or sand. Copper offers another barrier; it emits an electric charge as the slugs pass over it, which stops them in their tracks – so look out for copper tape or plant collars or scatter copper coins around the plants. Alternatively, offer the slugs some bran – they'll tuck in enthusiastically, but it swells inside them so they lose their appetite for your lettuces.

If you're still being besieged, set traps for these sneaky slitherers. Bury jars up to their rims around vulnerable plants and fill them with diluted beer. Slugs like a bit of a tipple, get drunk, fall into the beer and drown, hopefully before they even reach your plants. They also like to gather under upturned grapefruit halves or melon skins, and so can be 'harvested' in the morning and disposed of. Do this by immersing them in hot water or by sprinkling

Slugs and snails won't come anywhere near copper strawberry mats, which are designed to allow the plants to spread whilst keeping the fruit off the soil.

Grit makes the going tough for slugs and snails, so they'd rather avoid it. Use it as a barrier, sprinkled around vulnerable plants.

salt on them that sucks them dry, seeming to dissolve them. Not pleasant, but effective. Don't put salt directly on the soil, though, as this will make it toxic to plants.

Another method of attack is to draft in the nematodes – *Phasmarhabditis hermaphrodita*. These are minute worms that are available by mail order. On arrival they should be mixed with water and sprinkled onto the soil, where they search out slugs and release fatal bacteria into them. The decomposing slug becomes a food source for the nematodes, which then reproduce. The slugs die underground within five days and the nematodes are effective for up to six weeks.

As a last resort, scatter slug pellets sparsely around vulnerable young plants, or water in a liquid slug solution. Pellets contain strong chemicals that can, if eaten in quantity, harm children, pets and other wildlife, so check the labels for those that are, relatively, more animal friendly. These products will generally contain ferric phosphate, rather than the more vicious metaldehyde.

SOIL DWELLERS

Chafer grubs, cutworms, millipedes and wireworms are all soil-dwelling pests that damage roots and vegetables. If you don't mind using chemicals, products containing metaldehyde will eradicate these without affecting root crops. A more ecological solution is to use beneficial nematodes. Mail-order suppliers offer nematodes that target specific species, working in the same way as those that target slugs (see above).

The larvae of pea and bean weevils and bean seed fly feed on roots at this time of the year, and by June the adults will have climbed up the plants and chomped notches out of the foliage. Leaves with wavy edges are a sign later in spring that these creatures are in residence; if you see the beetles, pick them off, or fill a watering can with a rose-spray spout with a solution of water and cigarette ends and sprinkle this over the plants every two days. If the leaves recover, it will have disposed of the culprits!

WELCOMING GARDEN GUESTS

Gardens and allotments are hugely benefited by native wildlife: some are pollinators without whom there would be no flowers or fruit, some aerate the soil, and others are the natural predators of garden pests. Encourage a natural balance in your garden and you'll find you've invited a wide variety of wildlife guests who are more than happy to feast on your aphids, slugs and millipedes.

The general rule for encouraging wildlife guests is to provide them with shelter, water and their favourite food. Spring is the perfect time to do this, as many animals will need help surviving the lingering wintry weather and finding food when resources are depleted. Leave some messy corners around your plot for guests to take up residence and perhaps even hibernate later in the year. These could be the compost heap, rotting leaves or other vegetation under logs, trees, shrubs or long meadow-like grasses. It can be fatal for hibernating or breeding animals to be disturbed, so be careful not to disturb any such homes before the weather warms up. Some creatures can be attracted by rather more architectural homes and there are many websites offering boxes for a range of creatures from bees, ladybirds and other insects to bats, hedgehogs, birds and toads.

Pollinating insects are attracted by brightly coloured flowers, so plant some near vegetables such as beans, peas and courgettes and they'll pollinate those too! Bees love sunflowers for their hundreds of tiny nectar-bearing flowers in each flower centre, and are also particularly fond of blue flowers.

Ponds planted with a variety of native pond and bog plants also prove attractive. For some, they are a habitat and/or food source; for others, they're a water source. If you don't have space for a pond, provide a birdbath instead. Keep an eye on these over winter, break up ice and top up bird baths with fresh water in cold or dry periods.

Native nectar-producing plants and flowers will also encourage wildlife. When you are planning what to plant come

spring, try to include flowers to encourage pollination and beneficial insects. A rule of thumb is to choose single flowers (not double, as they often don't produce nectar) that are sweetly perfumed, such as honeysuckle, buddleia, lavender and foxgloves. Some insects, such as bees, are particularly attracted to blue flowers.

BATS

Every evening bats dine on midges, moths and aphids. They're also partial to crane flies (daddy longlegs), whose larvae, leatherjackets, can devastate your lawn. To encourage them, provide bat boxes with grooved 'bat ladders' and slotted entrances at the bottom. Site them in clusters of three or four, all pointing in different directions, about 4–5m (12–15ft) above the ground near or in trees, making sure the entrances are clear. Bats can take several years to decide to take up residence, but in the meantime, make sure they can't get under your roof eaves and into the attic of your house where they could cause havoc.

BEES

Bee populations are on the decline, so it's important to encourage these great pollinators into gardens and allotments. You can attract them by planting their favourite nectar-producing flowers, such as honeysuckle, foxgloves and aquilegia. They generally go for native plants, but particularly blue flowers and fragrant plants such as lavender, thyme and mint. You can also offer a home to solitary bees by making piles of hollowed-out stems or cardboard tubes with a diameter of between 2 and 8mm in a secluded area of the garden, or drilling similar-sized holes in fences or posts.

Invite bees into your garden with a beehive. You won't need much space, but in return, the bees will pollinate your flowers and provide you with delicious honey.

Invite other helpful insects to take up residence. Straws or holes drilled into blocks of wood or fences make five-star hotels for bugs, and nesting boxes sited sensitively will encourage birds to move in.

Putting in a pond is a great way to encourage wildlife. Frogs, toads and other amphibians, may take up residence as well as beneficial insects such as dragonflies. Birds will visit and feed on some insect pests.

BEETLES

Beetles are carnivores: their larvae live in the soil, feeding on underground pests. As adults, flying beetles prey on ants and grasshoppers, whilst underground beetles like nothing more than a meal of slug eggs, slugs, snails, lacewings and maggots. Leave a few untidy corners and the beetles will come; they love living under rocks, old leaves, rotting logs and mulch.

BIRDS

Birds keep the insect population down, eat weed seeds and sometimes small rodents and snails. They like trees and shrubs for shelter, berry bushes and 'meadow' areas of un-mown grass. Nesting boxes positioned in trees in a secluded place will encourage them to breed (see page 57). They also love water, so they'll come to a pond or splash in a birdbath. Feed them in the spring and early summer while they are rearing their young and in the winter with seeds, nuts and fat balls. Add a bit of chilli powder to their nuts and fat balls – the birds won't mind but squirrels find it too hot to handle, so it will stop them stealing their meals. If you encourage birds into your vegetable garden be warned that you will need to net your crops to stop them helping themselves.

DRAGONFLIES

As well as being a beautiful addition to the garden, dragonflies and their close relatives, damselflies, are some of the fastest flying insects in the world and expert at keeping the flying insect population under control. They mainly zap up mosquitos, flies and gnats, though they have been known to eat butterflies and moths, which keeps down the larvae that damage plants and crops. Dragonfly larvae will eat mosquito larvae. Dragonflies need water: that's where they lay their eggs and live as larvae for up to two years. So put in a natural pond and include a variety of native pond and bog plants.

FROGS AND TOADS

Both frogs and toads chomp into slugs, small snails and insects. Like many amphibians, frogs and toads spend most of their life on land, so lure them into your plot with damp homes for shelter. They'll consider long grass, compost heaps, log piles and nooks and crannies under the garden shed, greenhouse or decking. They need water both to breed and as a home for their tadpoles. If you want to encourage frogs to breed, you need a fish-free pond planted with a variety of native water and bog plants. You'll also need to provide a 'beach' so the young can make an easy exit once they mature into froglets. It's illegal to take frogspawn from the wild, but neighbours who have breeding frogs in their ponds may be delighted to give you some.

FLYING INSECTS

Most flying insects devour both green and black aphids and their larvae – and any other slow-moving vegetarian pests such as leaf-hoppers and caterpillars. The most useful include ladybirds, lacewings and hoverflies, which look a bit like very fast, skinny wasps. Encourage them with places to overwinter in, such as hollowed-out straws or holes drilled into fenceposts.

HEDGEHOGS

From spring to autumn hedgehogs are busy feeding on slugs, snails, caterpillars and millipedes. As winter approaches, provide a box filled with dried leaves (not straw, which could injure them) and covered with soil. Position it in a secluded spot far away from areas of activity, such as the compost heap or the house. If the box is disturbed at any time, they may decide to depart, which could prove fatal. Even in the summer, be sensitive, if they don't feel safe, they could leave, even abandoning their young.

SLOW WORMS

It's an honour to have these legless lizards, often mistaken for snakes, in your garden. A priority species under the UK Biodiversity Action Plan, it is illegal to kill or injure slow worms, which can live up to 54 years. They'll love to take up residence in your compost heap or under rotting logs and will happily munch on your slugs and snails.

BEGINNING TO BURGEON:

Early Summer

THE END OF MAY HERALDS ASTONISHING VERDANT GROWTH AND THIS IS THE SEASON WHEN EVERYTHING IN THE GARDEN REALLY GETS GOING. EVEN IN A YEAR WHEN SPRING IS SLOW IN STARTING, IT IS NOW THAT NATURE WILL CATCH UP ON ITSELF. YOUNG PLANTS SHOULD BE LOOKING VIGOROUS IN EARLY SUMMER, SO THE CHALLENGES IN THIS SEASON ARE TO ENSURE THEIR CONTINUED HEALTHY GROWTH AND DEVELOPMENT, AS WELL AS TO SOW NEW PLANTS OUTDOORS AND PROTECT THEM ALL FROM UNWANTED GARDEN GUESTS: WEEDS AND PESTS.

Pretty and perfumed

◁ A tripod of sweet peas doesn't take up much garden space yet it makes a pretty focal point and its perfume attracts the pollinators. It's also a flower cutter's dream: the more you cut, the more they flower!

Colourful crops

▷ Flowers might make the veg patch look pretty as a meadow, they're also the most enjoyable (and probably more cost effective) crop. Grow some cutting flowers in your patch for guilt-free snipping to take indoors.

The promise

◁ Peas, beans, courgettes and tomatoes will begin to flower – each bloom a potential 'fruit'. Let the pollinators do their work and your harvest will soon be on its way.

Food for free

▷ Now's the time you'll begin to see the fruits of your labours. The crops will have come on so fast it's hard to believe they were merely seeds a few weeks ago.

Classic beauty

▽ Artichokes lend statuesque structure to the garden whilst also producing delicious culinary treats.

FERTILISERS

Goodies in the soil gradually get leached out by the rain or in densely planted gardens they can be used up by competing plants, so to be able to continue cropping generous harvests and cutting a succession of fresh flowers, you will need to replenish the nutrients.

Plants should be provided with the best soil possible to get them off to a good start. Ideally you should improve what you have by digging in compost or manure in the autumn (see page 100), to allow them to further break down in the winter frosts so the soil becomes more workable. The aim is for the soil to have a soft crumbly texture that lets plenty of air, water and nutrients reach the plant roots. However, if you didn't do this in the autumn, all is not lost as you can do it now too. But try to dig in the nutrients as early in the spring as possible, to give them time to further break down and work their way into the soil.

In theory, with a good soil base the plants shouldn't need any more fertilisers throughout the growing season, but if you do add some in early summer and continue to do so as the plants grow and fruit or flower, you are more likely to get bumper crops and bountiful blooms.

Fertilisers broadly break into two groups: organic and inorganic, and it's up to you which you prefer to go for, depending on whether or not you want an organic garden. If you are growing fruit and vegetables, though, it is clearly more sensible to use organic fertilisers to produce chemical-free food. The vital ingredients of any fertiliser are nitrogen for green leafy growth, phosphates for root and shoot growth and potash for flowering and fruiting.

ORGANIC FERTILISERS

These natural fertilisers are slow acting, working over months rather than weeks. This group includes compost and manure, bone meal, seaweed and fish, blood and bone. As well as providing nutrients, organic fertilisers improve the soil structure. Slow-release fertilisers are organic types such as hoof and horn and bone meal, which degrade slowly to release their nutrients. The rate at which they do this depends on soil temperature, so as the soil warms up, they release more nutrients, just when the plants need them for their main growth period.

INORGANIC FERTILISERS

Fast-acting chemical fertilisers are made up of combinations of nitrogen, phosphates and potassium and can be delivered in many different ways: as granules or as a powder that is worked into the top few inches of damp soil, as a solution that is watered into the ground, or as a spray. Generations have relied on Growmore, or National Growmore (its original name), which was formulated during the Second World War to encourage bountiful home-grown harvests. Since then, a plethora of inorganic fertilisers have become available, often developed for different kinds of plants.

Controlled-release fertilisers are granules coated with a porous material that allows the minerals to gradually leach out into soil. The length of time that inorganic fertilisers continue to be effective can be controlled by the thickness of this coating.

HOW TO USE FERTILISERS

Fertilisers should be applied closely following the manufacturer's instructions. They can be delivered in number of ways:

As a base dressing – fertiliser is incorporated into the compost when potting on or when planting.

As a top dressing – fertiliser is applied on the soil surface around the plants, usually in spring to give the plants quick-acting growth stimulation.

By watering on – liquid feed is watered onto plant roots. This is mainly used in greenhouses and for container plants.

By foliar feeding – a diluted solution is sprayed or watered onto the plant's leaves, where absorption is fastest. This is a quick, emergency treatment for correcting nutrient deficiencies or can be used as a supplementary feed.

Comfrey can be rotted down into a rich nutritious organic fertiliser. It's also a pretty plant with decorative garden appeal. But be warned: it can be invasive!

MULCH

A layer of mulch is much more than a decorative covering to make your borders look neat. It also helps the soil retain moisture, keeps weeds in check, protects roots in the winter and prevents the fruits of low-growing crops such as strawberries coming into contact with the ground. Some mulches even help to improve the nutrient levels in the soil and act as deterrents to pests such as slugs and snails.

The best times to mulch are early summer, when the soil is warm and has not yet begun to dry out, or in the autumn before the frosts. The advantage of late spring and early summer, though, is that this coincides with planting, so the soil will have been prepared and thoroughly weeded.

BIODEGRADABLE MULCH

Almost anything organic can be used as mulch – grass clippings (but apply them thinly and avoid those from a lawn that has recently been treated with weedkiller), leaf mould, wood chippings, compost and straw. They don't all look especially pretty, but they become less obvious as they break down over the months, improving the texture of the soil and releasing nutrients.

Biodegradable sheet mulch is an excellent solution for strawberries, to keep the fruits off the soil.

Bark chippings make an inexpensive, attractive mulch which eventually biodegrades, improving the quality of the soil.

Coconut fibre helps to retain the moisture in the soil as sweetcorn grows and develops through the long hot summer.

An easier option, especially for city dwellers, is to use one of the rather more decorative bagged mulches such as bark and cocoa shell. Cocoa shell, derived from the cocoa plant, is attractive, smells like chocolate and, once laid, should be watered well to release the natural sticky substance that binds the shells together, making a protective matting that plants can grow through. This is not a good choice for dog owners, though, as chocolate is poisonous to their pets.

Biodegradable sheet mulch, made from cornflour, is water-penetrable and comes in a roll, which makes it easy to apply and less messy. Just roll it out over the newly dug-out bed in early summer and cover it with soil, then make holes in the sheet where you want to plant through. By the end of the season the sheet will have started to biodegrade, and simply needs to be dug into the soil.

NON-BIODEGRADABLE MULCHES

Gravel, grit and small slate paddle stones can also be used as a more decorative mulch. Although these do not biodegrade, they can help to lighten heavy clay soil, or be used for rockeries or gravel gardens. A more workmanlike option is to use plastic sheeting and weed-control fabric, which can be spread over beds and plants planted through slits in the material. Both materials are effective for weed control, but are more appropriate for the allotment or productive gardens as they are not aesthetically pleasing.

How to use mulch

If you are using sheeting as a mulch, lay it after you have prepared the soil and before you begin planting in early summer. If you are scattering mulch around plants, do so once they are in place and rake over a 2cm (1in) layer. Be sure to leave a small gap around the crowns of the plants to avoid the mulch causing them to rot in wet weather.

WEEDS

There's no getting away from it, there will always be weeds in the garden, and if you're going to provide a lovely environment for your plants, then the weeds are going to like it too. So, rather than resenting the impossible pursuit of a weed-free garden, see it as just part of the gardening process and make it your friend: a kind of therapy to help you unwind, to enjoy being outside, a chance to keep a close eye on your plants and spot potential problems early on.

Technically, there's no such thing as a weed: it's just a plant you don't want growing there. Live near sycamore trees and you'll find no end of tree seedlings in the garden, which you'll be pulling up as weeds. The one inescapable truth about weeds, though, is that if you don't keep on top of them, you're heading for trouble because they'll soon take over.

Generally, garden weeds fall into two categories: annual and perennial, and although all need to be removed at every opportunity, the way you do it is slightly different depending on which you're dealing with.

ANNUAL WEEDS

If you don't get on top of annual weeds at this time of the year, you're in danger of losing the battle later in the summer. They are spread by seeds, which might already be in the soil, having been dispersed by last years' weeds, and so may be incorporated in any compost or manure you've brought into the garden (see Compost, page 102), or they may have arrived in your garden on the wind, or been brought by birds. Your job, as far as possible, is to stop them germinating, and if they do, and they grow into small plants, to get them out before they go to seed and start the whole cycle again. At the height of the season, when growth is fast, or if you go away for a couple of weeks and the weeds grow into larger plants, prioritise any that look in danger of going to seed.

Here's your annual weed battle plan:

Mulch after planting (see page 66) – a layer of mulch deprives weed seeds of light and moisture, so many can't germinate or seedlings die off.

Hoe bare soil between plants and slice the weeds off and up onto the soil. Do this regularly using a sharp-bladed hoe on a sunny, dry day and the displaced weeds can be left on the soil surface in the sun to wilt and die.

Pull them out by hand as soon as they appear. Most annuals come out easily, root and all, but any that leave parts of their roots behind should be carefully dug out using a weeding tool or hand fork to stop them re-growing. Weeds come out of damp ground more easily than dry, so water the soil before weeding during dry periods.

Common annual weeds

Chickweed
Fat hen
Groundsel
Hairy bittercress
Knotgrass
Red deadnettle
Scarlet pimpernel
Shepherd's purse
Spurge

These persistent weeds are much more stubborn than annuals as they spread by various methods through their root systems, so if the root isn't completely removed, it just goes ahead and re-grows! Some perennial weeds are more difficult to conquer than others but all need attending to throughout the year whenever they make an appearance.

The idea is to eliminate as much of the plant as you can and weaken any survivors over the years with continued bombardment! You have two strategies: to dig up as much root as possible, or to regularly cut down green growth to weaken the plant. A last resort is to treat the leaves of individual plants with a systemic weedkiller that then works down into the roots.

Here's how to treat weeds with different types of roots.

Tap roots, such as dandelions and plantains, should be prised out with a dandelion weeder if they're small enough. For larger ones, starting 30cm (1ft) away from the weed if you can, dig down and around the root with a trowel or hand fork to loosen the soil until you can pull it out completely. Never let these perennials go to seed. Dandelion clocks might look very pretty, but each one releases hundreds of seeds. If you don't have time to dig out the root, chop the plant down until you do.

Perennial weeds

Tap roots
Dandelion
Dock
Plantain

Creeping roots
Buttercup
Creeping yellowcress
Ground elder
Nettles

Bulbil-type roots
Oxalis
Lesser celandine

Climbing weeds
Bindweed

Deep-rooted weeds
Japanese knotweed
Mare's tail

Japanese knotweed

Ground elder

Hairy bittercress

Creeping roots, such as nettles, pull up pretty easily, though even tiny left-behind pieces will re-grow, so use a garden fork to lift them if possible. If that is too disruptive to the surrounding plants, lift what you can, and if they re-grow, keep the foliage cut down to ground level to weaken the plant, then dig over in the autumn and remove any remaining roots. In a non-organic garden, really stubborn established nettles can be killed with weedkiller in the autumn. Pull up any young plants as soon as they appear before they develop their root system.

Bulbil-type roots, such as oxalis and lesser celandine, have tiny seed-like bulbils attached to delicate roots, which are part of the plant's propagation system. Dig, rather than pull, these out using a hand fork.

Climbing weeds, such as bindweed, can be almost impossible to remove entirely as they are entwined with other plants and roots. Pull up as much as you can and extract any young bindweed as soon as it appears before it has time to entwine itself around your plants, which it does remarkably rapidly, and to weaken its growth. Once you have cut back the garden in autumn, you could untwine any bindweed and gather it together before using a weedkiller.

Deep-rooted plants, such as mare's tail, provide the greatest headache and are almost impossible to totally eradicate, so it's more a matter of doing what you can to keep them under control. Their roots can grow down to a metre or more, so if you're starting your garden from scratch, dig deep to remove

Dandelion

Hedge bindweed

Stinging nettle

the roots. If that's not a practical proposition, you might have to resort to systemic herbicides that work through the plant down to the roots. Use it on a still day and protect other plants by making a shield around the weed made of a box or large plant pot with the bottom cut out. Mare's tail is one weed that can weaken even the most organic of gardeners.

Japanese knotweed is a particularly worrying clump-forming weed that has been identified by law as a pest species and if you find it in your garden, you need to be very careful in the way you eradicate it. It grows to over 2m (6ft) high every year and has roots that are so deep you'd need to dig down 3m (10ft) to uncover them all. If you chop at the roots and leave even the smallest pieces in the soil, they will simply regenerate. If you have just a few stems, the best way to weaken the plant is to use very sharp secateurs to carefully cut down the stems as they appear. Next, apply systemic weedkiller to each stem. This should weaken the plants and may even eradicate them over a period of time. If you can't eradicate them, call in a Japanese knotweed specialist.

CHEMICAL WEEDKILLERS

Most of us would rather not use chemical weedkillers, but if you've tried everything and you still have areas of persistent perennial weeds, they might be your only option. Choose your product according to your problem and space: non-selective weedkillers kill everything in sight; selective ones kill some plants but not others, where weeds can be targeted. This is difficult to do in a mixed border, so use weedkillers with care, if at all.

There are two types of weedkiller: those that kill on contact, and so-called systemic weedkillers that work their way down to the root and kill the whole plant. Various chemicals are used, but the most common garden weedkillers usually contain glyphosate. Most are sprayed on; others are applied to the leaves of individual plants to kill, say, persistent weeds growing through favourite plants or in a densely planted border.

If you plan to spray, choose a still evening when there's no wind to blow the chemicals around the garden. Shield the plants you want to protect from the weedkiller by placing a box or large plastic flower pot with the bottom cut out around the weeds and then spray within this shield. Alternatively, cover up favourite plants with plastic sheets cut from a bin liner.

Once the soil is warm enough – which could be any time between April and June, depending on where you live and the weather conditions of a particular year – you can sow seed directly into the ground outdoors. This saves the time and effort of preparing seed trays, pricking out and hardening off before planting out. Most native and hardy plants can be planted outside, though the timing and method for each can be slightly different (see the A–Z section, pages 108–183, or follow the instructions on the seed packet).

PREPARATION

Ideally you will have dug over the soil and forked in well-rotted compost or manure during the autumn (see page 100), so much of the hard work and preparation has already been done. In early spring, it is sensible to cover the bed with horticultural fleece or black plastic to warm up the ground ready for planting. In late spring and early summer, choose a still, dry day to rake over the soil to a fine tilth, picking out any weeds, stones, old roots or other debris as you go.

GET SOWING

Mark out the position of the seed drills in the beds using pegs and strings placed at the correct spacing for the crop, following the instructions on the seed packet. Now, make the drills, which means indenting the soil surface to make a groove to plant the seeds in. Depending on the size of the seed and the depth at which it needs to be planted, you can do this by either pressing a bamboo cane along the length of the string, or by using the edge of a hoe. Water the drills then sprinkle in the seed, sparingly and evenly. Very small

Seeds sown directly outdoors appear in dense drills. They'll need to be thinned out to allow space to develop and mature.

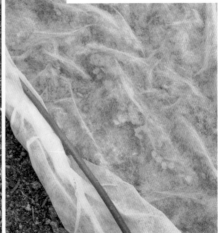

Use horticultural fleece to protect young seedlings from frost and enthusiastic birds who see them as tasty morsels.

Keep thinning out salad leaves as they grow, but don't waste them. They make a delicious addition to the summer salad bowl as baby leaves.

seeds can be difficult to separate and end up being sown in clumps. To avoid this, if they are not pelleted, the seeds can be 'diluted' by mixing with sharp sand. Lightly rake soil over the seed to cover, then mark each line with a label noting the name of the crop, variety and date planted. If there's any chance of frost, cover the drills with a sheet of thin fleece or some cloches.

If you're growing fast-maturing crops such as lettuce or salad leaves, you might want to sow seeds in every other line, or even less, and then plant in between them at two-week intervals so you have a longer, more manageable harvest period.

THINNING

When the seedlings of small-seeded plants appear, they will be overcrowded, so thin them out to give the stronger ones left behind enough space to grow and mature. (See the A–Z Section, pages 108–183, or check the instructions on the seed packet for the correct spacing between particular crops.)

BIG SEEDS

Big seeds such as runner beans or courgette seeds can be planted directly into their final position once the weather has warmed up. Again, sow them according to the instructions on the seed packets, observing the recommended spacings.

PLANT SUPPORTS

Many climbers or heavy-headed flowers will need support as they blossom and burgeon through the summer months. These supports range from simple bamboo canes and wooden stakes to various metal ones in a range of sizes designed for different plants and situations. Climbers offer the biggest challenges because their stems are not strong enough to be self-supporting. At boundaries, trellis can be fixed for climbers and ramblers, but you may prefer to grow beans, peas and other such crops in beds where they are easier to harvest, or to provide a vertical feature. In these situations wigwams, obelisks or a run of crossed poles with a horizontal pole running along the top can offer support as well as look good.

COPPICED PEA STICKS AND BEAN POLES

Before bamboo canes were imported to our shores, gardeners used naturally coppiced willow, hazel and sweet chestnut as pea sticks and bean poles. These are still available as a renewable resource from well-managed forests. Coppicing is the traditional craft of repeatedly cutting broadleaved trees down to the ground to encourage them to send up lots of new shoots, which are then harvested between January and May when they reach various sizes. If you'd like to use these, check out on the internet if there's a forest near you, or a supplier who can dispatch these to your area. Order as early as you can, because once they're sold out, you'll have to wait until the next year.

Twiggy pea sticks are only available early in the season so check out your local forest now. Look after them properly and you'll be able to reuse them for about five years.

Check the eventual height of pea and sweet pea varieties on the seed packet before making up support frames.

Runner beans can be grown on cane wigwams, or on 'racks' with the canes set wide apart to allow you to walk between them to harvest.

Willow is graded in diameter and sold by lengths of 30cm–2.4m (1–8ft). Twiggy-topped hazel is sold at 1.5m (5ft) as pea sticks, whilst longer and knottier bean poles are sold at about 2.4m (8ft) tall. These coppiced products are knobblier and stronger than canes, which makes them better at withstanding strong winds and easier for plants to cling to. They usually taper and curve at the top, making them good for arches and beanpole racks.

SETTING UP BEAN SUPPORTS

Bean supports need to be set up before planting to avoid root damage. Choose bean poles 2.4m (8ft) tall and 2.5cm (1in) in diameter and push them as far into the ground as possible. For a wigwam, set the poles 45–60cm (18–24in) apart in a circle and tie them together at the top using garden twine. For a rack of crossed poles, begin by marking out the positions. You need to be able to walk between the rows, so set the poles 60cm (24in) apart with 30cm (12in) between each pair. Start making the rack by putting up the end pairs in their marked positions. Next, lay the horizontal pole across the top. Use garden wire or twine to secure them in position. Now make up the rest of the poles in pairs between the two outside pairs. If you disassemble the rack at the end of the season and store it indoors, it should last for five years or more.

PEA STICKS

Allow 20 pea sticks for a 1–1.3m (3–4ft) run. Push them into the ground either side of the seedlings, leaving about 15cm (6in) between each one.

Rows of beans growing up supports can provide height and structure to the garden.

If you're short on space, you could even grow just one beanstalk up one cane.

It's a heartbreaking but familiar sight in early summer; just as your plants are putting on lush new growth, to find a plethora of tiny garden denizens arriving in the garden, chomping leaves and sucking sap, or discover that some fungal infection is weakening or rotting your plants.

Our natural reaction might be to zap them with insecticide or fungicide before they decimate our crops, but as you kill those aphids, caterpillars and weevils, you also destroy beneficial insects such as bees that pollinate the flowers and ladybirds that would make a good job of noshing aphids. Quite apart from those ecological factors, many people like to grow their own for the very reason that it's one way of guaranteeing insecticide-free food.

For anyone used to using chemical pesticides, the ecological route can seem painfully ineffective at first. The reason for this is that nature takes her time. Take aphids, for example. As temperatures rise, they arrive in their millions; if you spray them with pesticides, they're gone in an instant, but if you can bear the tension, leave them, and gradually you're likely to find the pest-infested plant covered in hundreds of ladybirds. That's because passing ladybirds stop to dine on aphids, lay eggs that hatch into larvae (which also eat aphids) and mature into more ladybirds. This establishes a cycle that should keep the aphids in check for the rest of the summer. The problem is, you can't be sure when those ladybirds are likely to stop by. It might be two days, it might be weeks! This is just one example of how organic gardening works. Choosing this route means it can take time to see results and you might feel it all rather depends on trusting to luck that the ladybirds will arrive before the aphids have ruined all the new growth. But nowadays there are options.

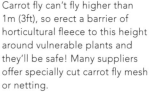

Courgette leaves are often mottled with mildew. This does not affect the delicious quality of the fruit and flowers, though you might be able to avoid it by spacing the plants further apart.

Carrot fly can't fly higher than 1m (3ft), so erect a barrier of horticultural fleece to this height around vulnerable plants and they'll be safe! Many suppliers offer specially cut carrot fly mesh or netting.

Hang up a wasp trap filled with something sweet and sugary such as fruit cordial, honey or jam to attract the pests. They'll be able to fly in but they won't be able to get out!

If you can't wait for nature to solve the problem you can internet-order reinforcement ladybirds to be sent by post, along with all kinds of other biological and ecological options. This puts effective organic gardening within much easier reach of us all, and is an idea that is being encouraged by governments, who are gradually withdrawing pesticides they deem dangerous to bees.

However, there are no hard-and-fast rules on how to deal with pests, and while gardening without any chemicals might be your ideal, if your crops are attacked by a particularly stubborn infestation you may have to resort to some form of localised chemical treatment. If you do need to go down this route, you'll find proprietary pesticides and fungicides in the garden centre. Some are labelled as eco-friendly.

10 STEPS TOWARDS AN ECO-FRIENDLY GARDEN

The key to keeping pests and diseases at bay the organic way is to think holistically and provide an ecologically well-balanced garden that will give you less need to administer emergency chemical treatments.

1 GIVE THEM STRENGTH

Strong healthy plants are better placed to fight pests and diseases, so it is important to offer them the best possible environment. A soil that has had plenty of good-quality compost dug into it will improve drainage and increase nutrient levels, whilst providing a good habitat for microbes that fight the development of fungi. Extra fertilisers, such as those in manure, or organic fertilisers, will also boost the plants' resistance to disease and provide extra resources to help them recover quickly from attack.

2 SUPPRESS WEEDS

Save all the nutrients in the soil for your flowers and crops by keeping the beds weed-free, then they don't have to compete for their fair share of nutrients. (See page 68.)

3 PLAN THE PLANTING

Try to include companion plants (see page 28) so plants can share nutrients such as nitrogen, and to help deter or distract insect pests such as aphids. Choose plant varieties that are resistant to fungal attack and plant them well spaced apart in a sunny position; good air circulation makes them less susceptible to mildew. Rotating your crops will reduce disease and fungal attacks on plants within the same family.

4 TREAT POWDERY MILDEW

Powdery mildew can be discouraged by spraying with water or a mixture of 60 per cent water to 40 per cent milk, or you can use a mixture of 1 tablespoon each of baking soda, vegetable oil and dishwashing liquid to 4 litres (1 gallon) of water. Some people also add a few drops of neem oil (see opposite).

5 CHECK FOR DISEASE

Cut out any leaves or part of the plant, including the roots, that is attacked by mildew or black spot, rot or any other fungus and burn it or tie it up tightly in a black plastic bag before disposing of it. Fungus spores can live in the soil for years, re-infecting subsequent crops. Check the susceptibility of individual crops and how to treat infections in the A–Z section (pages 108–183).

6 SET UP BARRIERS

Stop cabbage white butterflies, moths and other flying pests laying eggs on crops for their larvae to dine on. Use physical barriers, such as horticultural insect netting and polythene. Some pests, such as carrot fly, can't fly higher than 1m (3ft), so you only need a barrier to this height around the bed, rather than cover the plants completely. Special carrot fly netting is available.

7 PICK OFF THE BUGS

Picking pests off plants is surprisingly effective and easy to do, and disposing of them early in the season can slow down their reproductive lifecycle and save you a lot of work and heartache later. Look out for early-arriving aphids around succulent buds and leaf shoots and squish them in your fingers. Check daily under cabbage leaves for the eggs and larvae of cabbage white butterflies, and under lily leaves for the eggs and larvae of lily beetles.

8 BRING IN THE PREDATORS

You can order endless natural predators over the internet, including different types of nematodes that can see off slugs (see page 55), vine weevils, wireworm and sawflies; chafers for leatherjackets (daddy long leg larvae that can decimate lawns); encarsia for whitefly; and ladybirds for aphids.

Make sure you buy from a site that sells only species native to where you live. For example, American species used for biological control might not have the desired effect in Britain, and vice versa, and could even harm the ecological balance. Biological control often uses live creatures and organisms, so open the packages on arrival and follow the instructions precisely.

9 BREAK OUT THE NEEM OIL

Neem oil is a natural substance produced by a relative of the mahogany tree (the *Azadirachta indica* tree), to keep itself clear of pests. It targets mealy bugs, moth larvae, beetles, leaf miners and caterpillars without harming bees, dragonflies and ladybirds. It is sprayed onto leaves and travels down into the roots, working its magic on any creature that eats any part of the plant. It works by disrupting hormones, affecting the females' ability to lay eggs, the larvae's ability to pupate, and preventing pupae maturing into fertile adults. The best neem oil is

cold-pressed and should be used in the dilutions recommended by the proprietor. It is also sometimes incorporated, ready-diluted, into biological horticultural soap sprays and bio-friendly insecticides. As a fungicide, it works better as a prevention than a cure. Neem oil has been used pharmaceutically for humans for centuries to no known ill-effect. However, as with any strong substance, natural or chemical, avoid using it if you are pregnant or wanting to become pregnant.

10 GET SPRAYING

Horticultural oils can be used to kill slow-moving creatures, basically by suffocating them, while fast-flying predatory insects that feed on them are rarely hit. There are three types: petroleum-based, vegetable-based and neem oil (see above). Petroleum-based horticultural oils are not eco-friendly, but you can use those that are vegetable-based. Do not spray them on any beneficial flying insects.

ACTION STATIONS:

High Summer

FABULOUS FLOWERS, THE FIRST OF THE FRUITS AND EARLY
VEGETABLE CROPS ARE REWARDS FOR YOUR LABOURS RIGHT NOW.
IT'S THE BEGINNING OF GARDEN BUSY TIME AS TEMPERATURES
RISE AND THE GARDEN FILLS WITH FLOWERS, FOLIAGE AND FRUITS.
FROM NOW ON YOU'LL BE HARVESTING, PLANTING INTERCROPS,
PICKING FLOWERS, PRUNING BACK AND BATTLING PESTS OF ALL
KINDS: CREEPING, FLYING AND FUNGAL.

Celebrate

△ What's not to love when the flowers are blossoming, the fruit is setting and the beans are swelling. Rig up some bunting in celebration of summer – but not just for show; as it flutters in the breeze, it will scare away hungry birds.

Bye bye blooms

◁ When you grow flowers as crops, there will be plenty to cut and plenty left behind to keep the garden pretty and attract pollinators. Deadhead any blooms that go over to encourage the plants to make yet more flowers.

Airy elegance

◁ Umbellifers, such as this *Ammi majus*, cow parsley, fennel and dill, have a wonderful stately wild-flower quality that looks wonderful in the garden and fabulous in a vase.

Keep cutting

▷ What could be more delightful than snipping a few stems of cosmos and dill on a summer's day to fill a jug or vase to take indoors or just leave on the garden table.

Sunny harvest

▽ Sunflowers are the very icon of sunshine. They're also surprisingly prolific, so cut one, two or a few to make a stunning long-lasting arrangement.

Salad days

◁ Cut your salad and herbs, such as this flat-leaved parsley, fresh from the garden, just when you need it.

Net profit

▷ Shield your harvest from garden guests who want to share just a little too much. Horticultural netting comes in several gauges – choose a fine one to protect against insects as well as birds.

High achiever

◁ Climbing squash not only look impressive but also make an excellent crop. Once ripened and cut, they'll keep for months.

Pretty peas

△ Don't be shy about harvesting peas. Crop them when they are young and succulent – they'll thank you by producing even more.

Colour value

◁ Vegetables can bring colour to the flower garden as well as the allotment. Plant red-veined ruby chard like this, or yellow chard, beetroot or purple-veined cabbages in any kind of garden for delicious, nutritious colour.

PROTECT THE PRODUCE

The problem with creating a well-tended eco-friendly garden is that the produce is as delicious for our wildlife friends as it is for us. Our garden visitors naturally think that what's ours is theirs, and given half a chance they'll make sure they get the first pickings! While we don't mind sharing some of our produce, there are limits. In midsummer your plot will be at its most productive, and it's frustrating to see all your hard work disappear before you get a chance to crop it. Here are some ways to limit the plunder.

CREATE BOUNDARIES

A solid wall or fence is a good start: it's amazing how small a hole even a large animal like a fox or cat can get through. So check your fences and make any necessary repairs.

Within the boundaries, netting offers good protection. Sold on rolls, this is wonderfully versatile in that it can be used to cover single small plants, or on hoops to make tunnels, draped over bean wigwams, or over head-height frames covering whole beds. Generally made of polypropylene, it comes in many sizes to deter different bird species (err on the safe side and choose the smallest), and several colours (black, green, stone or translucent) to suit your environment. You can buy kits with all you need, including tools to put up the nets, as well as fine mesh to protect crops from insects.

PUT UP SOME BUZZ LINES

Some birds, such as pigeons, can get sneaky when it comes to nets, bouncing up and down on them until they can reach down to the tallest crops. Foil them by criss-crossing lines of string diagonally across the top of the frame. They'll stop the pigeons getting in, but are not stable enough for them to stand on. As a deterrent you could make the buzz lines from silvery ribbon.

A windmill whirring in the wind, or the gentle notes of chimes will deter the birds from visiting your crops.

Wildlife will run from flapping clothes that whiff of humans – even pretty hats on canes!

Flappy flags in contrasting colours hoisted high on canes are enough to scare the birds. They look decorative in the garden too!

Plastic hoops make a great frame for netting. Chose a fine-grade net for insects; a larger one for birds.

USE FLAPPERS AND SCARERS

Most creatures are alarmed by sudden movement, so anything that flaps makes a cheap and easy scarer. String up flags, bunting or shiny old CDs or DVDs, or 'plant' colourful pinwheels. Wind chimes will also make enough noise to alarm birds and small mammals. Alternatively, invest in a battery operated, sonic, animal repellent. Some of these work by using high-pitched sounds that humans can't hear and animals can't bear; others use distress sounds or noises made by predators. Old-fashioned scarecrows still offer a great solution. They not only look like humans (well, to wildlife they do!), but if you dress them in old shirts (preferably unwashed) and tuck human hair in their pockets, they'll smell like humans too, which deters many animals.

MAKE A SMELL

Many small animals are not too partial to strong smells emitted by some herbs and members of the allium family, so plant aromatic herbs such as mint, thyme, tarragon, oregano, artemisia or yarrow and alliums such as onions, garlic and chives near your crops. If you don't have the space, scatter essence of lion dung pellets around the crops. For legal reasons, these can't be labelled as deterrents, so they're sold as fertilisers! However, not many creatures, including squirrels, deer and foxes, feel welcome in gardens they think are inhabited by extremely large cats. Scatter the pellets 7–10cm (3–4in) apart – wear gloves to prevent human scent tainting them.

OFFER THEM THE TASTE TEST

Many animals, including squirrels and rabbits, are none too keen on fiery tastes, so in small areas sprinkle chilli around the roots of vulnerable plants. This is not a good idea if you have children or pets, but it could be a solution if you have a rabbit problem and want to grow beans. They just love to nip off those beanstalks at the base.

COLLECTING SEED AND
REFRESHING THE COLOUR

Summertime, and the garden is at its most beautiful. Lush, decked with flowers and burgeoning crops – this is the reward for all our work so far – but by the beginning of August, it begins to look like the party's over. Flowers are replaced by seedheads, leaves lose their lushness and the plot starts to look scraggy and overgrown. It may seem like the cutting garden has little to offer now, but there are some clever ways to keep the colour going until autumn, when everything gets a new lease of life.

DEADHEADING

As far as the lifecycle of the plant is concerned, the whole point of flowering is to produce seed to create new plants. Once that's done and the seed is ripening, there doesn't seem much point in producing any more flowers, so the plant directs all its energy into maturing those seeds. But you can delay this process if you keep cutting the flowers as they bloom; the more you cut, the more the plant produces in its determination to seed. At this time of the year, you also need to deadhead any flowers that have begun to go over, both to encourage new blooms and to keep the plants looking tidy. Check the plants daily and use a sharp pair of secateurs to cut off any flower heads that are past their best.

However much you snip away, though, there comes a point at the end of the summer when the plant comes to the end of its flowering season, after which it will slow down its flower production. This is the point at which you need to allow some flowers to go to seed, especially if you want annuals such as nigella to self-seed, or you want to collect seeds for the next season.

Sunflower seeds provide essential nutrition for birds. Each flower head is so astonishingly abundant that just one or two left in the garden will keep the birds fed for several months.

As the main flower season draws to a close, look for late summer- or autumn-flowering plants to enliven the gap left by those that are past their best. Here, cosmos fills a patch of bare earth.

COLLECTING SEED

Collecting and using your own seed may produce surprising results compared with seed bought from commercial suppliers. Firstly, some seeds will not reproduce true to their parent plant as they often revert back to the original species. Secondly, they may germinate erratically. Commercial producers collect, treat and store seeds in ideal conditions to ensure that as many germinate as possible. Amateur gardeners don't have those conditions, so if you do collect your own seeds, regard the process as an experiment: if some germinate, then so much the better. Having said that, the seeds you collect will be ready-acclimatised to your garden, and so may well produce surprisingly successful results.

Plants produce seeds in many ways: in capsule-like seedcases, within berries or as large fruits, to name some of the more obvious. The easiest seeds to collect are those that the flower puts on show, such as in the heads of sunflowers. They'll tell you when they're ready to harvest because the flower head will bend down to 'look' at the ground! If you don't want to miss this turning point, or share ALL the spoils with the birds, you can tie a paper bag around the sunflower head to catch the seeds as they fall. You can do this with much smaller flowers, too! Some of the easiest to collect and germinate are those that are encased in seedcases that turn from green to brown, which indicates they are ready to be harvested. Use a sharp pair of secateurs to cut off whole seedheads, then shake out the seeds into a paper envelope and label with the plant name and date. Keep the seeds in the shed or greenhouse until you're ready to use them. Some can be planted straight into the ground in autumn; others should be saved for germination in the spring – refer to the A–Z section (pages 108–183) for information on each variety.

INTERPLANTING

There are some wonderful flowers that bridge the gap between the main summer flush and autumn, and you can use these to plant between still-flowering or fruiting plants to give the garden a short burst of new life. The classics include endless pink and purple aster varieties, including the iconic Michaelmas daisies, Love Lies Bleeding (Amaranthus), Cosmos, dahlias, gazanias and zinnias. They should now be grown on sufficiently, showing buds, and ready to replace annuals that are past their best.

Once you've harvested all the seed from the summer-flowering plants, dig out these old plants and add them to the compost. Dig over the soil where they once grew, ready for plants that flower into the autumn and provide a last splash of colour.

EXTENDING THE HARVEST

The key to getting the most produce out of your limited space is to make use of every spare pocket of soil, quickly re-colonising areas that have been newly vacated by harvesting and avoiding losing produce such as lettuce and rocket by letting it bolt. Careful planning of your plot early in the year should have taken all this into account, but it's difficult to think of everything at once, and even if you do, the vagaries of the weather can scupper the best-laid plans. But by now, with the season well under way, there may be bare earth where some crops have failed, or even if they haven't, you may be able to spot places where you can squeeze in new ones. There are several ways to do this.

SUCCESSIONAL SOWING

Fast-maturing salad crops, such as lettuce, rocket, radicchio, beet and cabbage (when used young) should be planted in succession. This means you need to plant just a few plants every two weeks or so to give you a chance to crop and use them all before they bolt. Mark out several drills but only plant in every other one. Some people sow two different crops at once, for example, a combination of lettuce and radish in one row; once these have been thinned out they have a manageable quantity of lettuce, and as you crop the radishes, you leave space for lettuce to grow and mature. Bear in mind that by high summer the lettuce will bolt even quicker than it did earlier in the year, this is because it's both warmer and there are more hours of daylight, so you need to be harvesting as soon as it looks ready. If you plan carefully, you can even get two harvests out of each sowing of these fast-maturing crops.

INTERCROPPING

You can make maximum use of space by planting smaller crops between larger ones. So, for example, you can plant courgettes under sweetcorn, which doesn't cast too large a shadow over the smaller crops while still young. Alternatively, you could plant smaller crops that don't like too much direct sunlight in the shadow of taller ones.

CATCH CROPPING

Similar to intercropping, catch cropping is a way of simultaneously growing fast- and slow-maturing varieties. Choose fast-growing varieties such as salad leaves, radishes and baby root vegetables such as baby carrots, baby beets, spring onions and pak choi and plant them between slower-growing crops, such as Brussels sprouts, kale, onions and parsnips.

INTERCROPPING COMBINED WITH CATCH CROPPING

If you're clever, you could get two harvests out of two fast-growing intercrops grown between the rows of a slow-maturing winter harvest like leeks.

There's room between the maturing squash to plant young red orach (a type of spinach) for a harvest that will continue well into the autumn.

As harvested crops leave bare earth, sow new ones directly in the ground between the rows to make the most of your available ground.

For example, you could sow a slightly thicker drill than normal of lettuce combined with radish between the leeks. Use the first lettuce and radish thinnings as baby salad leaves and then, around four to six weeks later, thin them again to harvest baby roots and more salad leaves, leaving enough space for the remainder to grow to maturity. By the time the lettuce and radishes are over, you might be ready to harvest a few baby leeks, leaving the rest to grow and fill the spaces left by the now-harvested salad crops for delicious autumn and winter harvests.

PREPARATION AND PLANTING

Each crop depletes the soil of nutrients and the more extra crops you squeeze in, the harder the soil has to work. Before re-sowing or planting in your beds, prepare the soil by removing all traces of the old crop and fork in extra compost to replenish the nutrients. Rake over the soil until you have a fine tilth, then plant the new crop following the description in the relevant section of the A–Z, or according to the instructions on the seed packets.

THE GLUT AND TIDY UP:

Autumn

THE DEWY MORNINGS OF EARLY AUTUMN REVIVE THE GARDEN, GIVING IT A WHOLE NEW VIBRANT LOOK WITH FLOWERS IN SHADES OF YELLOW AND ORANGE. RATHER MORE SURPRISINGLY, PINKS AND MAUVES ALSO BURST INTO BLOOM ALONGSIDE THE AUTUMN FRUITS, VEGETABLES AND BERRIES JOSTLING TO BE HARVESTED. IT'S A RACE AGAINST TIME NOW TO GATHER IN, STORE AND PRESERVE ALL THE CROPS BEFORE THE FIRST FROSTS SPOIL THEM. ONCE THAT'S DONE, THERE'S NO TIME TO REST ON YOUR LAURELS, AS IT'S SWIFTLY ON TO TIDYING UP THE PLOT FOR WINTER AND EVEN GETTING AHEAD ON PLANTING UP SOME OF NEXT SPRING'S CROPS!

Nature's store

▷ Pumpkins and squash in all their variety are ready for the picking in autumn. They make great-value crops as they can be stored in a cool dry place for months.

Pick the blooms

▽ Autumn brings a late flush of extrovert flowers. Plunge them straight into a bucket of water as you wander round the garden picking them.

Natural sculpture

△ The weird and wonderful shapes of squashes are at their full-blown best in autumn. Keep them off the dewy ground by propping them up on boxes, bricks or plastic sheets or they will begin to rot.

Hips and haws

◁ Old-fashioned roses may only produce one flush of flowers in the summer, but in the autumn, they bestow the garden with their fabulous rosehips and haws.

Autumn mists

▷ The early morning autumn light is breathtaking as it falls on the dewy garden. A welcome relief after the parched, overgrown look of late summer.

Harvest time

▷ Fruit trees are astoundingly abundant at this time of year, with branches so laden with fruit that there's plenty to crop and plenty left to share with the wildlife. The sweet musky smell of apples, pears and plums scent the autumn air.

Purple prize

△ Pretty Michaelmas daisies dress the garden at this time of year. Part of the aster family, there are plenty of varieties to choose from shades of almost blue to pink and purple.

HARVESTING AND STORING

Growing your own fruit, flowers and veg is one thing, but it's knowing when and how to harvest and store your produce that will make all the difference when it comes to enjoying the full fruits of your labour.

TIMING IS EVERYTHING

Many crops will all be ready to harvest at the same time, rather than being continuous croppers, so think about this when you plant. There is no point in sowing serried ranks of lettuce if you can't eat more than two or three a week, as they will just bolt and be wasted. So, just sow a few every fortnight, or team up with neighbours and agree to swap some of your lettuce for their tomatoes. Equally, keep an eye on your crops to see when they are ready to harvest. In spring, monitor the growth of any early bird candidates such as radishes, lettuces and strawberries and gather them in as soon as you can. As the season progresses, the harvest will accelerate and it will become increasingly difficult to keep up, and then you will be hit with the abundance of autumn when it is a race to get everything in before the first frosts. Each entry in the A–Z section gives details as to how and when to harvest individual crops.

STORING THE HARVEST

Most fruit and vegetables start to deteriorate as soon as they are cut. Some can be frozen (see page 98), otherwise you can store or preserve the harvest using methods that have been relied upon for centuries. Different crops must be treated in different ways, so here are the basic methods.

FLOWERS

These cannot be stored once harvested, although some varieties can be dried (see page 187).

FRUIT

Soft summer fruits, such as strawberries, currants and summer raspberries start to appear midsummer, while blackberries, tayberries and loganberries arrive later, but they can all be treated in the same way. A sunny day or weekend can ripen these fruits extraordinarily swiftly, so they need to be harvested before they go over. If you have a glut, you can freeze them (see page 98) or turn them into jams, jellies, cordials or curds (see page 210).

Firmer tree fruits, such as apples and pears, can be turned into jams and jellies. If you want to store these fruit whole, wrap each one individually in newspaper or acid-free white tissue and pack them into boxes on well-ventilated shelves. They can also be blanched and frozen (see Freezing, page 98).

VEGETABLES

Legumes, such as beans and peas, were traditionally dried for winter use, but this isn't practical in our busy modern lives, so instead freeze gluts immediately. Courgettes do not store well and should be eaten within three weeks or made into soup for freezing. Tomatoes need to be eaten once they are ripe. If you can't keep up, make them into chutney. Green tomatoes that failed to ripen before the threat of frost, can also be harvested and made into green tomato chutney (see page 224). Alternatively, speed-ripen them on a sunny windowsill or in a paper bag with a very ripe banana. (The bananas release ethylene, which will speed up the ripening of the fruit.)

Root vegetables, such as potatoes, carrots and beetroots (but not parsnips, which can be left in the ground until you need them, and in fact taste better after a frost) can be stored in boxes of sand over winter. Check over each root for disease, rot or fungus and dispose of these – they cannot be stored as they will spread disease. Before storing the healthy roots, cut off their leaves. Choose a large wooden box and put in a layer of sand and lay the vegetables out in a single layer so that they don't touch each other. Add another layer of sand and then another layer of vegetables and so on. Check them occasionally over the winter and discard any that show signs of rot. You can also use these vegetables in chutneys and pickles (see page 210).

Newly-harvested shallots will keep for months if hung in a cool dry room (left), and already, the winter greens are under way (right).

Onions, garlic and shallots should be left to dry out on trays in the sun as soon as they are lifted. Once the skin and leaves have turned papery, store them hung up in some old tights, or plaited French onion-seller style in a well-ventilated, cool dry place. They can also be used in pickles and chutneys (see page 210).

Squashes and pumpkins with hard skins and firm flesh can be stored in a cool dry place until spring.

FREEZING

Now that many homes have a freezer, this has become a popular and easy way to preserve the harvest for later in the year. Some fruits and vegetables need to be blanched before being frozen, which basically means plunging them into boiling water or steaming them for a few minutes (see box below). This stops the enzyme activity that naturally causes the decay of plant material, which can survive freezing temperatures but not boiling points. Different fruits and vegetables need different blanching times, depending on their density.

Pack the blanched vegetables into freezer bags or boxes and label them clearly, stating what they are and the date on which they were frozen. Most can be frozen for up to 8 months.

Soft fruits like raspberries and blackberries can just be popped straight into a polythene bag or boxes and put in the freezer, but if you want to use them later as individual fruits, freeze them on a baking sheet, spaced apart, then box or bag them up once they are frozen.

Currants – red, white or black – should be fast-frozen prior to being stored in the freezer. Leave them on their strings and pop them into the fast-freeze section. If you take them off their strings before freezing, they will lose some of their juice and could rupture. After a couple of hours, use a fork to strip them off their strings, then pop them into a polythene bag or box and return to the freezer for longer-term storage.

> ### Three steps to blanching
> 1 Prepare the vegetables by choosing only perfect specimens and topping, tailing and chopping where relevant.
> 2 Bring a pan of water to boiling point. Plunge in the vegetables and boil for the recommended length of time.
> 3 Immediately plunge into cold water to stop the cooking process and drain.
>
> Blanching times:
> **Beans**: runner – 3 minutes
> **Broccoli** – cut into 2.5cm (1in) pieces, 2 minutes
> **Peas** – shelled, 1½ minutes

THE AUTUMN DIG

Autumn is the best time to properly dig over your soil. Once the crops are harvested and the spent plants are cleared away and composted, you are left with sections of bare soil that can be worked before the wet weather makes this job more difficult. A good digging over will aerate the soil, breaking it up and introducing plenty of oxygen, which helps bacteria to break down organic matter and release nutrients. Once the soil has been turned over, let the worms do their job of further breaking up and aerating the soil. Winter frosts will also help to break up clods of earth, making the soil more workable come the spring. Ideally do this digging between October and December, before the frosts and the worst of the winter weather. Do not dig over soil when it is heavy and wet, as you can damage its structure, creating poor drainage and aeration.

At the same time, you should remove any weeds, roots and stones and dig in humus, such as compost or any other green manure (see below), to introduce extra nutrients and provide a good environment for the natural soil bacteria to work, ready for planting in the spring. If you do this year on year, your soil will continue to improve over time, aerating clay soil and bulking up sandy soil.

IMPROVE THE SOIL

How well your plants grow depends to a large extent on the quality of the soil they're grown in. It's their source of water, air and nutrition, so the aim is to provide the best balance you possibly can. Bear in mind that in a lush cultivated garden the plants are more than likely to be far more crowded than they would be if they were left to nature, and so they'll need to be fed with more goodies than they would if left to go wild.

If you inherited a garden with poor soil, you might find it helpful to buy and dig in some good topsoil. Make sure this is premium grade from a reputable dealer, is free from roots and has been properly sterilised so you're not importing weeds, seeds or fungus spores.

The best soil improvers are well-rotted manures and compost (see page 102), which can be forked into the soil.

Green manure

If you are not planning to plant any winter vegetables, you could sow green manure seeds. These grow over the autumn, taking up any nutrients left in the soil that would otherwise be washed away over winter. Then, in spring, before planting the next season's crops, you dig the green manure plants (or their frosted remains) back into the ground, roots and all, where they rot down, releasing the nutrients back into the soil and improving its workability. Seed suppliers sell mixed packets, many of which include legumes (peas and beans) that fix nitrogen in the soil, and winter tares or winter grazing rye, which grow all through the winter. Green manure can also be used earlier in the year between crops as a weed-suppressing mat.

Composting

The autumn cut-back produces a huge amount of vegetation that can be put straight onto the compost heap to decompose, ready for replenishing the soil.

Dig plenty of compost into beds at this time of year so the frosts can further break it down over the winter.

There is no need to dig deep down into soil that has already been cultivated. Forking it through to a depth of 37cm (15in) is sufficient to incorporate organic matter to improve the soil structure. Alternatively, you can leave a 5cm (2in) layer of manure or compost on the surface, effectively like a mulch, so the nutrients leach down during the winter rains, or worms work them into the soil. You can then dig them into the soil in spring.

HORSE MANURE

Well-rotted horse manure is an excellent nutrient-rich soil improver. You can buy it inexpensively in bags in garden centres, which will have been rotted down well enough for immediate use, or you can bag it up yourself from obliging local suppliers. If you're buying from a local farm, riding stables or door-to-door salesmen, check over the manure for suitability. It should have rotted down sufficiently so that you can't see any wood shavings or straw. If the manure is too fresh it will scorch your plants, so it pays to check it thoroughly and not be impatient! If you have space, you can add some to your compost heap for an extra burst of nutrients.

MAKING COMPOST

Whether or not you're adding topsoil, in the autumn, when you're digging over the soil, it's a good idea to add humus, which is basically any partially decomposed vegetable matter such as manure, leaf mould, bark or wood chippings that can be used to improve the soil (see page 100).

Compost is available from garden centres, and there are a range of types available for different purposes (see page 40). However, if you need a general-purpose compost, the cheapest and most satisfying version is home-produced compost.

Experienced gardeners wax lyrical about their compost heaps, which are whole eco-systems that provide an environment in which heat, moisture, bacteria and wildlife combine to speed up the rotting process, and all the energy given off by bacteria, fungi and nematodes can raise the temperature to 75°C (167°F).

If you have a large enough garden, make at least two, if not three, heaps of compost in a hidden corner. One heap should contain fresh cuttings and

prunings, then once that has rotted down over about a fortnight, you can turn it over into the next heap. After a month, transfer it to the third where it can be left to rot down into sweet-smelling, nutrient-rich compost to put on the garden. You'll need to turn this third heap regularly using a garden fork to speed up the composting process.

If you don't have space for three compost heaps, one will do, but if space is really at a premium, invest in a composting bin. There are many to choose from, including rotating bin versions so the compost can be turned (though, in practice, these can be very heavy and difficult to turn). Choose a bin that you can open at the bottom so you can easily shovel out the oldest compost as it matures to use on the garden.

Compost enthusiasts and scientists talk about hot composting and cold composting and ratios of carbon to nitrogen, but in essence, organic material just wants to decompose. For most of us, it's much easier to think in terms of green waste from the kitchen and garden, which needs to be interspersed with brown waste such as cardboard boxes, paper, or dead and dried leaves and stems in order to break down efficiently. The brown waste helps to introduce oxygen and stops the green material from decomposing into a dense oxygen-starved sludge. Always start your bin with a layer of coarse material, such as plant stems, to encourage drainage through the heap, then build up layers of garden waste above it.

There are some provisos as to what garden waste you can add to your compost bin. Hot compost heaps should be hot enough to kill off weed seeds, but composting with just one heap or bin is more likely to result in cold compost, which won't destroy them. So if you want to dispose of weeds on your heap, pull them up before they set seed. If you're too late, get rid of weeds that have gone to seed at the local recycling centre, otherwise, you'll have your work cut out next year battling those nicely nurtured weed seeds! You also need to beware any perennial weed material, such as roots and shoots, that can regenerate. It's better to be safe than sorry, so kill these off before composting them. This is easily done – just pack them into a black plastic bag, seal it, then leave it for a month or so in a sunny position until a sneak peek shows the weeds no longer look like roots, by which time they'll be safe to add to the compost (see Weeds, page 68).

You can get a compost heap started in autumn as you clear the site after the harvest, although it won't be ready for over a year, as compost rots faster in summer than winter. Heaps started in spring should be ready by the autumn of the same year. To ensure material rots down efficiently, make sure the contents of the bin are roughly 25–50 per cent green materials, such as grass clippings, kitchen waste (peelings and uncooked fruit and veg), and annual weeds, with the remainder being made up of brown material – prunings, dead leaves, paper, etc. Never let one type of waste dominate, as it will affect the texture of the finished compost.

The compost is ready when it is dark brown and has a crumbly, soil-like texture.

THE BIG TIDY UP

The big autumn tidy up is immensely satisfying! This is the time to cut back all that astonishing summer growth that has gone to seed and become unruly and to get the garden back under control for the winter. It's also important to be meticulous about garden 'hygiene'; so be sure to burn or otherwise permanently dispose of any diseased plant material, scrub out pots, scrape off spades, disinfect secateurs and other blades, and give nest boxes a good clean to stop any spread of disease.

CUT BACK

Uproot annuals that are over and use a good pair of sharp secateurs to cut down perennials that are past their best. Overgrown shrubs, except spring-flowering evergreens, should be pruned back and tied securely to stakes or trellis with soft garden string so they are not damaged in winter gales. Many are then re-pruned in the spring to encourage growth, though exactly how and when depends on the species (see A–Z Roses, page 175). Give other shrubs a once over, and remove any damaged or diseased stems or branches to keep infections at bay. Once the garden is clearer, dig out and dispose of any perennial weeds (see page 68).

SWEEP UP

As the weather turns, the leaves begin to fall, and one of the biggest jobs in autumn in most gardens is sweeping up falling foliage. Even before the main leaf drop, check for any leaves that have fallen around plants that are susceptible to black spot, leaf mould or any other fungal infection. Start clearing away all leaves as soon as you can; if they are not removed now they will soon be covered up by the many more leaves when the main leaf fall happens and their spores will become stored in the earth, waiting for spring when they can spread their diseases. If your local council allows bonfires, burn any infected leaves, otherwise bag them up and dispose of them with the rubbish. Do not put any leaves with mildew, black spot or any other fungal disease onto the compost heap.

Freshly fallen, healthy leaves should be swept up as they drop as these make excellent composting material. You can put them on the compost heap if you wish, but a better use is to pack them up in black plastic sacks, add a little water if they are dry, then pierce the bag with a garden fork a couple of times to create a few air holes, then loosely tie up the bag. Find a corner of your plot and leave the bags there for up to two years, by which time you will have beautifully nutritious leafmould. If you have space – and a lot of leaves – it is worth creating a cage out of chicken wire and piling up the leaves in it. Just add water if it gets dry, and leave it to decompose. The open heap method takes the same amount of time as the bags – it's a slow but worthwhile process!

Make sure you scrub your tools after the big tidy up to remove traces of weed seeds and any fungal spores.

Forking over all the beds will aerate the ground ready for digging in the compost. Year on year, this will improve the quality of your soil.

WASH UP

Boring, maybe, but maintaining good hygiene around your plants is the best way to keep disease at bay. Pots and containers should be scrubbed out at the end of the year to remove any fungal spores, mites, pests or weed seeds. Scrub them with a stiff brush or wire wool, then soak them in a solution of 10-parts water to one-part household bleach to kill off any lurking diseases. Thoroughly rinse them out then leave them outside to dry. Birds' nesting boxes should be cleaned too, to remove any mites, parasites or disease. Dispose of the old nesting material, scrub the box using warm water and washing-up liquid, then rinse it out with boiling water to kill any organisms. Allow the nest boxes to thoroughly dry out. Bean poles and pea sticks should be taken out of the ground, scrubbed and stored, dry, in the garden shed.

KEEP THEM WARM

Before the first frosts, lift tender perennials such as dahlias, acidanthera, pelargoniums and fuchsias, which won't survive the frosts, pot them up and store them under cover, along with any potted tender plants. Put them in a greenhouse or unheated conservatory, or on a cool windowsill indoors. If you have large pots that can't easily be moved, keep the roots of the plants warm by wrapping the containers in bubble wrap, and cover the plant with horticultural fleece, which is available in sheet form, as bags that can be slipped over the top of plants, or even as zip-up jackets for larger plants.

PLANTING SPRING BULBS

The astounding transformation from a bare garden to one that is vibrant with colour in the spring has to be one of the greatest joys of living in a climate with seasons. But to get this display, you need to get busy with bulbs in the autumn.

Bulbs don't take too kindly to hanging around, so buy them when you're ready to plant and get them into the ground within a week. Choose large, firm bulbs that will be mature enough to flower in the first year, and have neither rotted nor dried out. Discard any that already have shoots.

Most bulbs like a warm sunny position in fertile, well-drained soil, but there are a few, such as erythroniums, scillas and bluebells, that will welcome a little shade.

Bulbs look best when planted in drifts, rather than as small groups dotted through beds. Dig out the chosen area to the correct depth (see box below), throw in some handfuls of blood, fish and bone and throw the bulbs on the ground. Plant them where they fall, positioning them so that they point upwards, then replace the soil and firm it down with the back of your hand. Water the bulbs in.

For smaller groups, you may like to plant the bulbs individually. It's easiest to do this using a bulb planter (see page 33), which you push into the ground to the relevant depth, twist and pull to remove the plug of soil, place the bulb in the hole, replace the soil, firm it down with your fists and water in.

Planting depths and times

A simple rule of thumb is to plant bulbs to a depth two to three times the size of the bulb itself. Each species needs to be planted at a slightly different time.

SPECIES	PLANT	DEPTH	FLOWER
Crocus	Sept–Oct	7.5–12.5cm (3–5in)	Feb–April
Snake's head fritillary	Sept–Nov	7.5cm (5in)	April
Crown imperial	Sept–Nov	20cm (8in)	April
Daffodils	Aug–Sept	10cm (4in)	March–April
Tulips	Nov	15cm (6in)	April–May
Hyacinths	Sept–Oct	10cm (4in)	April–May
Grape hyacinths (Muscari)	Sept–Oct	10cm (4in)	April–May

AFTERCARE

The bulb is the plant's own store cupboard filled with nutrients that will lie in wait, ready to be tapped for next year's growth, and in the very centre are the beginnings of a flower bud. The plan for any gardener is to conserve the supplies and build them up – bulbs don't need rich fertiliser, but if you like you could give them a specialised bulb fertiliser whilst they are in flower so they don't deplete their own reserves too much.

As soon as the bulb has finished blooming, cut off the flower so that the plant doesn't invest any energy in producing seed. The leaves draw energy from sunlight, replenishing the bulb, and so should not be cut down or tied up, but left to soak up as much sun as they can. Only cut them down to tidy them up once they've died down naturally, which might not be until July for daffodils and tulips. There should be no need to water the bulbs unless there's a prolonged dry spell.

SNOWDROPS

Planting snowdrops as bulbs isn't usually successful because they dry out very quickly. The solution is to plant them 'in the green' – which means when they're in leaf and after flowering. You won't be able to buy them like this until late winter or early spring, but as there will be plenty to be planning at that stage and you may forget, make a note in your New Year's diary now.

When you buy snowdrops in the green, they'll come in a large clump. To plant them, choose a partly shaded, moist position and dig in garden compost first. Dig a large trench deep enough to accommodate the bulbs with the leaves at surface of the soil. Divide off a row of snowdrops, carefully untangling their roots. Place them at one edge of the trench and fill in around them with multipurpose compost. Now divide off another row and repeat. Carry on like this until all the snowdrops are planted and press the soil down firmly. Water. Do not trim away the leaves until they die down, at which point cut them off with sharp secateurs.

PLANTING BULBS IN CONTAINERS

Containers of bulbs are brilliant because, once planted, if you feed them in spring they will produce flowers for you year after year.

Bulbs need free drainage, so in autumn plant them in a mixture of three parts John Innes No2 mixed with one-part grit. Position them in the soil at three times their depth and one bulb apart. Water them regularly during active growth and once the shoots appear, start to feed them with liquid tomato feed every seven to ten days to promote good flowering. Stop feeding them once the foliage begins to die down.

Once they've finished flowering, put them in a secluded part of the garden and check the pots to make sure they never completely dry out. Then, next year, when the shoots appear, you can bring them out again, and put them on show on the patio or front garden.

A-Z

plant profiles

WHETHER YOU WANT TO GROW YOUR OWN IN POTS ON THE PATIO,
AMONGST THE FLOWERS IN THE BORDERS, OR IN A DEDICATED VEG
PATCH, YOU FIRST NEED TO WORK OUT WHAT YOU WANT TO GROW IN
THE TIME YOU HAVE AVAILABLE. BEFORE MAKING UP YOUR MIND,
CHECK THROUGH THIS HANDY GUIDE TO GROWING EVERYONE'S
FAVOURITE VEGETABLES, HERBS, FRUITS AND FLOWERS. EVEN IF YOU
DON'T HAVE TIME TO GERMINATE FROM SEED AND JUST WANT TO BUY
A FEW YOUNG PLANTS TO GROW ON, IT WILL GIVE YOU AN OVERVIEW
OF WHAT'S EASY, WHAT'S A TOUCH TRICKY AND HOW MUCH YOU CAN
EXPECT TO HARVEST.

AUBERGINE

Solanum melongena

DIFFICULTY RATING: MEDIUM

Beautiful, glossy and delicious, aubergines are expensive to buy in the greengrocer, which could make them a worthwhile crop to grow. But 'could' is the operative phrase. Native to India, where temperatures top 40°C (over 100°F), aubergines need a long hot summer to produce any fruit, and since British summers are anything but reliable, growing them can be a bit of a gamble.

Generally, your best bet is to germinate and grow them in a greenhouse, although even then, if it's a drizzly summer, the lack of a decent amount of sunny hours could lead to disappointing results. More optimistically, if you live in a milder part of the country and the summer happens to be long and hot, you might even be able to grow and harvest your own aubergines outside. That said, there are ways of increasing your chances of success. Instead of sowing seed, you could use grafted plants, which have been bred to be more hardy than most aubergines.

SOWING

Aubergines need a long growing period, so start them off any time from January in the greenhouse if you're going to cultivate them under glass. If you live in milder climes and you want to plant them outside in the summer, you'll need to start them off in the greenhouse in early March. They need a temperature of 18–21°C (65–70°F) to germinate. If you don't have a heated greenhouse, you could germinate them in a propagator (see page 34) on the conservatory windowsill, or in the airing cupboard. Start by soaking the seeds for 24 hours, then sow them in trays, modules or small pots. If you are germinating in the airing cupboard, bring them out into the light as soon as the seedlings appear. Prick them out into 9cm (3½in) pots, and once the roots fill those, onto final 23cm (9in) pots, filled with container compost if you are growing them under cover.

GROWING

If you want to grow aubergines outside, choose a warm, sunny, sheltered site. Harden them off once the risk of frost is over (see page 44), and meantime, warm the soil by covering the planting position with cloches for two weeks. Plant them out 60cm (24in) apart. Keep the young plants covered with cloches for at least two weeks until they are fully acclimatised. Water regularly, and once the fruits begin to swell, add a soluble fertiliser to the water every fortnight. Stake the plants to give them support as they grow. If you're growing regular-sized aubergines, allow five fruit to set then pinch out the rest. You can allow smaller-fruiting aubergines to set more fruit. Regularly mist greenhouse-grown aubergines.

HARVESTING

Cut the fruits when they are around 15cm (6in) long and have shiny skins, or, if you're growing smaller varieties, according to the supplier instructions. If you find yourself with a surplus, they can be used to make delicious preserves, see page 226 for Aubergine and mustard pickle, or even used in flower arrangements!

(See Summer table arrangement, page 195.)

PROBLEMS

Outside, look out for **whitefly**, which can be controlled with biological sprays based on plant oils, or **aphids**, which can be squished between your fingers, or controlled with ladybirds, which can be ordered online (see page 77). In the greenhouse, you'll also need to look out for **red spider mite** or **two-spotted mite**, which can be a problem in hot dry conditions. You might not see them, but you might notice fine webbing like miniature spiders' webs, and the leaves will drop. Control this by spraying with biological control such as *Phytoseiulus persimilis*.

BEANS, BROAD

Vicia faba

DIFFICULTY RATING: EASY

The most compelling reason to grow your own broad beans is that you can pick them young at their succulent best and enjoy a vegetable that is almost unrecognisable from the often tough and hoary version available in the shops. Harvested early enough, they can even be cooked and eaten whole in their pods!

Broad beans can be planted straight into the ground any time over the autumn and spring months, so they are a good choice if you don't have a greenhouse or much space for germinating seeds under cover. Dwarf varieties can be planted in containers – perfect for urbanites even if they have little more than a patio or a balcony. This is a tried-and-tested crop, dating back almost eight centuries to when they were first grown in the Mediterranean.

BASIC TYPES

There are three classifications of broad beans.

Dwarf are bushy, early cropping plants, reaching a maximum height of 45cm (18in): ideal for growing in pots or under cloches.

Longpods, with their pods of up to 35cm (15in) in length, offer the best yield, are hardy and crop early.

Windsors are not hardy and mature later than the other varieties but are generally considered to offer the best flavour.

SOWING

If the winters are mild in your area and you have a sheltered spot, you can plant the hardy varieties directly into the ground in mid- to late autumn, for harvesting about 26 weeks later. Don't leave it too late in autumn, though, as you'll want your seedlings to be at least 2.5cm (1in) tall before the first frosts arrive. Protect them against the worst of winter with cloches or fleeces. A safer bet is to sow them straight into the ground in March and cover them with cloches for extra protection until the seedlings are established.

In autumn, choose a sunny spot and prepare the soil by digging in well-rotted compost. A week before sowing, rake in a general fertiliser and if the weather is dry, water it in. This may well encourage weeds to grow (they like the goodies too), so thoroughly weed the area before sowing. The beans need to be planted 5cm (2in) deep and 20cm (8in) apart in double rows with walking space between each set of double rows. If you want a long harvest, plant a few plants every three weeks. The taller varieties need staking.

GROWING

Keep the ground weed-free either by hoeing it regularly or mulching it with bark chippings, which has the added advantage of retaining moisture in the soil. Unless early spring is unusually dry, the broad beans shouldn't need extra water until the flowers start to form. When the first beans appear, pinch out the top 7.5cm (3in) of stems both to encourage the beans to mature earlier and to discourage black bean aphids. At the end of the season, when all the beans have been harvested, cut off the stems, add them to the compost heap and dig the roots

back into the ground to replenish the soil.

COMPANION PLANTING

Plant summer savory nearby to lure those pesky black bean aphids away from your beans.

HARVESTING

You can start harvesting broad beans when the pods are 5–7.5cm (2–3in) long, at which stage they can be eaten whole, pod and all. For shelling, pick them when the beans are just about beginning to swell – leave it any later and you risk tough beans. Gluts can be added to the Quickalilli pickle on page 229.

PROBLEMS

Slugs and snails, see page 54.
Aphids, see page 76.

BEANS, RUNNER

Phaseolus coccineus

DIFFICULTY RATING: EASY

Native to Central America, runner beans were brought to Britain in the seventeenth century. Although Native Americans had been eating runner beans and their roots for about 2000 years, the plant was initially prized in Europe for its decorative red flowers and used to adorn gazebos, arbours and pergolas. It wasn't until the mid-eighteenth century that Philip Miller, head gardener at the Chelsea Physic Garden, thought to cook them!

Pretty, abundant and easy to grow, you get a lot of veg for not much effort from runner beans, so they're a great choice for beginner gardeners. About 12 weeks after you press those pretty mottled pink beans into compost, the vines will have grown to about 3m (10ft) and you'll be harvesting from early summer right up to the first frosts. Given a good summer and attentive care, each planted bean can produce up to 1kg (2lb) of delicious fresh green pods.

SOWING

Runner beans can be germinated under cover from late spring and then planted outside as small plants in their final position once all risk of frost has passed. You can plant them directly into the ground in late spring/early summer, although this will result in later cropping.

Runner beans prefer a sunny position in soil that has been prepared either in autumn, with plenty of well-rotted manure, or in spring with good-quality compost.

The beans need to be planted 5cm (2in) deep, 25cm (10in) apart in rows 45cm (18in) apart so you can walk between them to make harvesting easier.

If you don't have a veg patch, plant runner beans at the back of flower beds or in containers. Choose a container at least 20cm wide by 25cm deep (8 x 10in).

STAKING

Provide each plant with a tall, sturdy cane or pole driven well into the ground – these can be arranged in tent-like rows or as 'wigwams', but allow space to 'get at' the inside beans to harvest them. Given a little encouragement, the plants will happily wind themselves up the pole, but pinch out the growing tip once they get to the top to encourage growth lower down. (See plant supports, page 74).

GROWING

Keep the beds weed-free and water well to help the flowers to form and the pods to swell. Mulching the bed will help preserve moisture in the soil while also keeping weeds down. Harvest while young and succulent, at lengths of 15cm (6in) to get them at their most tasty and to encourage the plant to produce more pods.

COMPANION PLANTING

One of the Native American planting combinations, the Three Sisters, runner beans were traditionally grown alongside maize (sweetcorn) and squash as part of a mutually beneficial trio of plants. The sweetcorn provides a natural support for the beans, which provides stability,

helping the corn stay upright in high winds. Low-growing squash provides an alternative mulch, keeping the roots of all the plants moist, whilst the nitrogen-fixing bean roots improve soil fertility.

Nitrogen-fixing runner beans are beneficial to more plants than benefit them. They'll thank you for planting them near aubergines and summer savory, but keep them clear of tomatoes, chillies, onions, garlic, shallots and kale.

HARVESTING

To keep crops coming, be prepared to harvest every other day in the height of summer. If you can't keep up with consumption, freeze the surplus or use in the Quickalilli pickle on page 229.

PROBLEMS

They can be infested by **black bean aphids** or fall victim to **mildew**.

BEETROOT

Beta vulgaris

DIFFICULTY RATING: EASY

Beetroot is hailed as something of a superfood now, which is quite a journey from its lowly position as the vinegary bottled vegetable sliced into limp post-war salads. Well-documented studies indicate that it lowers blood pressure and improves exercise performance. It is also said to lower cholesterol and stabilise blood-sugar levels, is packed with antioxidants to help protect the immune system and folic acid, which helps tissue growth.

Whether or not you believe the claims, it's a pretty good vegetable to eat. Home grown and roasted, it has a delicious flavour and a fine texture. It is not difficult to grow (though germination can be a bit tricky) and if you plan carefully, you'll be able to store your excess and be eating it all through the year. As well as our much-loved, deep red, globe varieties, beetroot can also be yellow or white and tapered or cylindrical in shape, which adds interest to a delicious mix of roasted vegetables.

SOWING

Each beetroot 'seed' is actually a tiny fruit containing several seeds. They're not quick to germinate, so soak seeds in water for several hours before sowing. To get a harvest from May through to the beginning of November, you'll need to make successive plantings at fortnightly to monthly intervals. You can start the earliest crops in late winter in a cool greenhouse, cold frame or windowsill before planting out, then in late spring you can sow directly outside.

Prepare an open sunny spot in the autumn, digging in plenty of well-rotted compost or manure. Warm the ground with cloches, then, 2–3 weeks before sowing, thoroughly weed the bed, and rake in some general fertiliser.

Place the seeds in the ground about 2cm (¾in) deep and 2.5cm (1in) apart, then mulch around them. When the seedlings are strong enough, thin to 10cm (4in) apart. Alternatively, sow seeds in drills, thin the seedlings as they appear, and keep thinning as the plants grow. Keep the seedlings protected by a cloche or horticultural fleece for 4–6 weeks after sowing.

GROWING

Beetroot needs regular watering, but just enough to keep the soil moist. If beetroot is overwatered it grows fabulously lush leaves, but if you under-water it could become woody and is in danger of splitting, especially if it rains heavily or you try to redress the balance by watering copiously.

COMPANION PLANTING

Beetroot is generally trouble-free and combines well with carrots, cucumber and lettuce, but also, because they take only 9–13 weeks to mature, are ideal for intercropping and catch cropping (see page 90). Plant garlic, chives onions and/or mint nearby to see off the blackfly to which beetroot is prone.

HARVESTING

Globe beets should be harvested any time from golf-ball up to cricket-ball size. Generally, early

salad varieties are cropped smaller and maincrop beets are left until they're bigger. As the season progresses, you can harvest every other one when small, leaving room for the rest to grow. Lift them carefully with a fork to avoid damaging the root, shake off the dirt and twist off the leaves down to a 5cm (2in) stalk – if you cut the leaves, they'll bleed. Any beets you can't cook now can be stored in single layers in sand, bottled in vinegar (see Harvesting and Storing, page 96), or used to make Allotment chutney (page 230) or Beetroot relish (page 234).

PROBLEMS

Beetroot can bolt or the roots can become woody, usually because of stress due to cold snaps or drought. Keep the soil moist to get the best produce.

CABBAGE

Brassica oleracea

DIFFICULTY RATING: MEDIUM

In theory you could grow cabbages all year, but in practice, they take up a lot of space – up to 45 x 45cm (18 x 18in) per cabbage – and occupy it for up to 35 weeks. Winter cabbages should be cut in November, after which they can be stored until March. In reality, with cabbage readily available in shops, most of us would probably rather grow them for one season, freeing up their corner for other crops over the rest of the year. Spring cabbages are the most worthwhile in that they are the smallest varieties and are planted in winter when there's space in the plot anyway. They are ready to harvest as delicious young greens by the end of February, but you can then look forward to harvesting them as they mature through spring and early summer.

TYPES

Cabbages are divided into three main groups according to when they are harvested.

Spring cabbages are small and conical. Seeds are sown in July and August, and planted out in September and October. Harvest from March to May.

Summer cabbages are usually ball-shaped, though some are conical. Sow from February until May – although early sowings should be protected with cloches. Plant out between April and June for harvest from June to October. **Red** cabbages are in this category.

Winter cabbages are large, round and dense, and can be green or white. The latter keeps for months. Crinkly-leaved **Savoy** is another winter variety. Sow in April and May, plant out in June and July and cut from October to March.

SOWING

Traditionally, cabbage seeds are sown into seedbeds rather than directly into position. Sow them 7.5cm (3in) apart in drills 1cm (½in) deep and 15cm (6in) apart. If you don't have room for a seedbed, germinate the seeds in modular trays, then pot them on until they are large enough to plant out into their final growing position. Or use them as an intercrop (see page 90). If they're sown more densely than their final spacing (check on the seed packet), harvest every other one to eat as salad leaves.

Cabbages like good firm soil that has been improved with manure or compost in the autumn, but don't plant them in a newly dug site; instead, tread it down and gently rake over. Don't plant cabbages on a site where brassicas have been grown in the past year.

GROWING

Once the cabbages have five or six leaves, they're ready to be transplanted into their final positions. Water them well the day before, then make a small hole for each plant, put the plant in and fill the hole with water several times (you'll see it drain away) before replacing the soil and firming it in. Keep the beds free of weeds and water well about every ten days.

COMPANION PLANTING

Plant rosemary, onions or garlic nearby to deter cabbage white butterflies.

HARVESTING

Cut the stem close to the ground with a sharp knife. If you score a cross in the stump of spring and summer cabbages, you can get another crop of small cabbages.

PROBLEMS

Caterpillars of cabbage white butterflies will chomp into leaves and **cabbage root fly** larvae eat roots. Net the plants to prevent butterflies laying eggs, or put brassica collars around stems to stop larvae getting to the roots. Check the underside of leaves daily for eggs or caterpillars.

Cabbages can get **club root**, a fungal disease that often attacks in acidic soil or in warm, wet weather. Affected cabbages must be dug up. You must remove the whole root without damaging it, to prevent spores being released. Avoid planting cabbages on the same site for five years.

CARROT

Daucus carota

DIFFICULTY RATING: EASY

You might want your carrots grown for the local village show to be large, long and perfectly formed, but if you're growing them to eat, shorter and sweeter is better – and definitely easier! Carrots can be fussy, demanding deep fertile beds of sandy soil, and the longer you want to grow them, the deeper this must be. There are three basic types: short rooted, which are sown early and mature quickly; intermediate types, which are good all-rounders; and long-rooted varieties, which are the super-model show types and not necessarily tastier.

Carrots like a light sandy soil that has been dug over the previous autumn but not enriched with manure or compost as this causes the roots to fork. In stony soil, grow short varieties to prevent stunted crops.

SOWING

Carrot seeds are minuscule and easy to sow too densely. Traditionally, gardeners mixed them with sand before sowing to break them up, but now you can buy easy-to-handle pelleted seeds. Sow them sparsely in order to reduce thinning out, which you want to avoid because the smell emitted by bruised leaves attracts carrot fly.

If you can start early varieties under cover, so much the better. Sow two or three seeds to a module and thin before planting out. Once they are large enough, plant out 5–7.5cm (2–3in) apart, otherwise, sow drills outside from mid- to late spring 2cm (½in) deep and 15cm (6in) apart. Thin the seedlings to 7.5cm (3in) apart.

Later carrot varieties are sown in late spring and take longer to mature. Check the seed packets and plant some from each of the early, maincrop and late-cropping varieties to harvest carrots from June right through to December, depending on the local climate.

GROWING

Rake the seedbed three weeks before planting, allow any weeds to grow then remove them by hand. Once the carrots are planted, either mulch around them or be meticulous with weeding so that you don't bruise the carrot tops, releasing their scent and attracting carrot fly. Keeping them weed-free gives them lots of space so their roots can develop nicely. Keep the ground moist for tender carrots; if you let it dry out too much and then overwater, the roots may split.

HARVESTING

Early varieties are ready to harvest after 8 weeks, which is around early June, maincrops from 10 weeks after sowing and can be left in the ground until you're ready to eat them. The carrots, especially if they are young early crop varieties, should be easy to pull up by hand. If the weather's been dry, this might be a little harder, so water the ground first. If maincrops are stubborn, lift them out with a fork. October is the time to harvest any remaining maincrop carrots and store them (see Harvesting and Storing, page 96), or cook into Curried carrot chutney (page 233) or Allotment chutney (page 230).

PROBLEMS

Carrot fly is enemy number one! The larvae of these insects tunnel and chomp into the carrot, turning the leaves bronze and making the root inedible. There are three ways to keep carrot flies at bay:

1 Try not to bruise the carrot leaves: the smell of the sap that is released is a carrot-fly magnet.
2 Companion plant with onions. Their smell repels carrot fly. If you don't have the space or don't want to grow onions, water carrots once a week with a dilution of Olbas oil (from the pharmacy). Use 3 drops to a 4-litre (1-gallon) watering can full of water.
3 Carrot fly can't fly higher than 60cm (2ft), so keep them out by making a barrier 1m (3ft) high all around the seedlings using polythene, specialist mesh, such as Enviromesh, or thin horticultural fleece.

CHILLI/SWEET PEPPER

Capiscum annuum

DIFFICULTY RATING: EASY

Chillies and sweet peppers are all just different varieties of the same plant that is native to South America. As they are sun-loving tender plants, they generally need to be greenhouse grown, though you might be able to harvest a good crop of outdoor peppers at the end of a long, hot summer in milder locations. Both chillies and sweet peppers are happy grown in pots, and if you don't have a greenhouse or space under cover to start them off from seed, buy young plants from the garden centre and keep them outdoors on the patio, bringing them indoors early in the season if a cold night threatens.

SOWING

Any time from early spring you can sow chilli and sweet pepper seeds in 10cm (4in) pots filled with moist good-quality seed compost. Keep to 21°C (70°F) until they have germinated, then gradually lower the temperature. If you don't have a greenhouse, you can use a propagator, or start them off in the conservatory or a light, warm windowsill. Once the seedlings are 2.5cm (1in) tall, prick them out into 10cm (4in) pots. Keep them watered in a sunny spot indoors.

GROWING

When the peppers reach 30cm (12in) tall, pinch out the growing tip of stems when they are 15–20cm (6–8in) tall to encourage a bushy habit. Once the danger of frosts are over, harden off the plants, and either transplant them into 22.5cm (9in) pots or plant them outside in the ground 38–45cm (15–18in) apart. While the nights are still chilly, cover them with a cloche. During the growing period, feed them every two weeks with general purpose fertiliser and water regularly.

HARVESTING

You can harvest peppers and chillies when they are still green, or leave them until they have turned to their ripened colour. Simply snip off the fruits with secateurs or florist's scissors. At the end of the season, when frosts threaten, cut the branches and hang them upside down in a dry sunny position to further ripen. They can also be used in pickles, such as Aubergine and mustard pickle (page 226) or Curried carrot chutney (page 233), or to add heat to Caballero salsa (page 237) or Garcia's green sauce (page 241). They also give a kick to fruity preserves such as Bramley apple and chilli jelly (page 245).

PROBLEMS

If you are growing them under glass, keep the greenhouse well-ventilated, otherwise the plants could be susceptible to fungal diseases.

Aphids can be a problem: either squish them between your fingers or enlist some ladybirds to deal with them (see page 76).

Whitefly suck the sap from the plants and can be dealt with in the greenhouse using *Encarsia formosa*, a tiny wasp (see page 49), which is available online from specialist suppliers or through garden centres.

COURGETTE

Cucurbita pepo

DIFFICULTY RATING: EASY

Courgettes are a brilliant beginner veg; they reliably produce a good crop and the more you pick, the more they obligingly bring forth. They also have fabulous showy edible flowers that look stunning in a salad or are delicious stuffed and deep fried! A member of the cucumber family that includes marrows, squash and pumpkins, this is a versatile favourite because you can pick the courgettes small when they're firm and flavoursome to eat raw, sautéed or roasted, or let them grow and use them stuffed with rice or mince as you would a marrow. The round varieties of courgette, rarely found in the shops, are particularly delicious, so these are well worth growing.

SOWING

In early May, choose a sunny spot and prepare it by digging out a hole for each plant that is about a spade's width, depth and height, about 90cm (3ft) apart, then fill them with equal parts soil and compost and dig in a small amount of general fertiliser. About a fortnight later, plant three seeds about 2.5cm (1in) deep and 2.5cm (1in) apart in the centre of each filled hole and cover them with a cloche until they have germinated and grown into seedlings. Thin them out to leave one strong seedling in the centre of each.

Alternatively, you can start the seeds off in compost-filled biodegradable pots either outside if the weather is warm (from late May), or under glass (from mid-April), then harden them off. When they're ready to go outside, just plant one, complete with its pot, into the centre of each filled hole.

Mulch around the plants to improve moisture retention in the soil and to keep the fruits off the earth. Courgettes also grow well in containers and, with their handsome leaves and bright flowers, can be very decorative on the patio. Plant three seeds in a container filled with good-quality compost and, once germinated, thin to just one strong seedling.

GROWING

Courgettes like to be kept moist, so water around the plants but not too near the crown, to avoid rotting. Each plant produces flamboyant yellow flowers, some of which are male, some female. The female flowers have what looks like a tiny courgette behind the petals whilst the males have a slim stalk. Sometimes all the first blooms are male – possibly to give bees and other pollinating insects the heads-up of where they are before they make the effort to produce both kinds of flowers. Once both males and females open, there should be no problem leaving the insects to do their pollinating job. However, if the female flowers start dropping-off, you'll need to collect pollen from the male using a cotton bud and transfer it to the female flowers.

Feed every fortnight with a high-potash liquid fertiliser once the fruits start to appear and swell.

COMPANION PLANTING

As part of the squash family, courgettes can be planted near runner beans and corn to bring

together the Three Sisters (see page 113).

HARVESTING

The more you harvest courgettes, the more they produce, so pick them when they are still small – around 10–12.5cm (4–5in) long – and at their most delicious. Collect any spent male or dropped female flowers, wash them and use them in salad or pasta dishes. Courgettes are quite prolific, so try preserving them (page 251), or adding them to Allotment chutney (page 230) or Quickalilli (page 229).

PROBLEMS

Powdery mildew is the most common problem when growing courgettes and is a sign that the plant is under stress, probably due to dry conditions. Mulching and regular watering will help avoid this.

CUCUMBER

Cucumis sativus

DIFFICULTY RATING: EASY

There are two types of cucumbers: greenhouse and outdoor. Greenhouse varieties are long and have smooth skins, while outdoor cucumbers are usually smaller and have rougher skins. The latter are known as 'ridge' cucumbers because they are traditionally grown along the ground on ridges of earth; greenhouse cucumbers are grown up canes.

SOWING

The seed of both types need to be sown in a propagator from March. The seedlings don't like their roots being disturbed, so sow them in 7.5cm (3in) pots (biodegradable are good as you can then pot on or plant out without disruption). Sow the seeds on their sides to a depth of 1cm (½in). Keep them at 20°C (68°F) away from direct sunlight until they germinate in 7–10 days, after which they need a minimum temperature of 15°C (60°F). Keep the soil moist. When they're big enough, indoor cucumbers can be planted in growbags 45cm (18in) apart. For outdoor cucumbers, once frosts are over, choose a sunny, sheltered, well-drained site and dig in plenty of rich compost. Warm the soil with cloches whilst you harden off the plants, then plant 90cm (36in) apart.

GROWING

All cucumbers need plenty of nutrients, so feed them every two weeks with a high-potash feed.

GREENHOUSE CUCUMBERS

Naturally, cucumbers have both male and female flowers, but if indoor cucumbers are fertilised, the fruit will be sour so you need to remove the male flowers. These are attached to the plant with a little stalk, while the female flowers have a swelling behind them that looks like a mini cucumber. Easier still, buy seeds that produce female-only flowers. Cucumbers love humidity, so damp down the greenhouse floors regularly, and protect them from direct sunlight to avoid scorching (see page 46). Train trailing types up 1.8m (6ft) canes to encourage more fruit and pinch out the growing tip once it reaches the top. Once the fruit starts to develop, pinch out side shoots to just two leaves after each fruit to encourage a more plentiful crop. Water around the cucumber plants regularly, avoiding wetting the leaves, as this encourages mildew.

OUTDOOR CUCUMBERS

These can be left to just trail along the ground. Once seven leaves have formed, pinch out the main stem to encourage more fruit-producing side shoots to develop. Outdoor, or ridge, varieties all have both male and female flowers and need to be pollinated, which can be left to the butterflies and bees. Water around the plants regularly as indoor types.

HARVESTING

You can harvest the first fruits of outdoor varieties twelve weeks after sowing until September, or into October with indoor cucumbers. Cut the fruits early in the morning using sharp secateurs. Delicious in pickles – try Quickalilli (page 229).

PROBLEMS

Powdery mildew is more prevalent in a humid atmosphere where the soil has been allowed to dry out. It starts on the upper surface of the leaves, but can spread to the underneath. Remove any affected leaves. If necessary, use a fungicide.

Whitefly will suck the sap of cucumbers, creating a sticky substance. Use a biological spray containing fatty acids. Indoors, use the parasitic wasp, *Encarsia formosa* (see page 49).

Cucumber mosaic virus is spread by aphids and gives the leaves a yellowing mosaic appearance, reducing the flowers and making fruit inedible. Buy resistant varieties, such as 'Bush Champion', 'Crispy Salad', 'Jazzer F', 'Paskia Fi', 'Petita' and 'Country Fair'. If plants show symptoms of the virus, destroy them to avoid spreading it.

GARLIC

Allium sativum

DIFFICULTY RATING: EASY

Nobody in Asia or the Mediterranean would dream of cooking a savoury dish without the addition of garlic. Quite apart from its characteristic flavour, it's been valued for its health-giving qualities since Ancient Egyptian times. Science has now caught up and verified many of the claims, which include its ability to reduce cholesterol and blood pressure levels and possibly prevent some cancers. It is anti-inflammatory, antioxidant, antibacterial and antiviral – quite an achievement for so small a vegetable! From a gardener's point of view, it's also easy to grow and a great pest deterrent, so it's widely used in companion planting.

PLANTING

Garlic is grown from individual cloves separated out from the bulb. Don't be tempted to pop in one from the supermarket – it could be diseased, dried out, or imported and so not suited to our climate. You're more likely to get better results from bulbs bought from a garden supplier, or saved from last year's crop. Traditionally, garlic is planted before Christmas because it needs a long growing season to produce decent-sized bulbs. Autumn planting is the very best option, giving the garlic time to develop a root system before winter sets in. This both helps it survive cold winters and gives it a good head start once the soil begins to warm up in spring.

Choose a sunny spot with fertile soil and incorporate a general fertiliser before planting. Garlic is susceptible to fungal infections. Bought cloves should have been treated against this by the suppliers, but you can give bulbs further protection and an energy boost by soaking them overnight in a soda-water solution made up of 1 teaspoon of baking powder and 1 teaspoon of liquid seaweed to 1 litre (2 pints) of water. Remove the papery clove covers because they can harbour fungal spores or mite eggs. Choose only the best cloves, then rub them with 100 per cent-proof vodka to clean off any pathogens the soaking missed and plant immediately. Plant each clove root end down at twice its depth, 15cm (6in) apart in rows 30cm (12in) apart.

GROWING

Keep the garlic weed-free and water if there are dry spells in spring or early summer. You won't need to water once the bulbs are well-formed, because this could rot them.

HARVESTING

Once the leaves turn yellow, the garlic is ready to harvest by carefully lifting out with a fork. The bulbs will then need to dry, so lay them out in a single layer in a well-ventilated place until the papery covers are dry to the point of rustling, then transfer them to ventilated containers. They add depth of flavour to preserves such as Tomato chutney (page 224), Aubergine and mustard pickle (page 226), Allotment chutney (page 230), Curried carrot chutney (page 233), Caballero salsa (page 237), Garcia's green sauce (page 241), as well as Preserved artichokes (page 248), Preserved

courgettes (page 251) and Drowned tomatoes (page 252).

PROBLEMS

Fungus can be a problem, although the risk can be reduced if you prepare the cloves well before planting (see Planting). However, if the leaves wilt and turn yellow, or become loose in the soil in wet conditions, they may have onion white rot. Lift one, and if there's a white fluffy coating on the bulbs, destroy it and don't grow garlic, onions or leeks in the same place for eight years.

LEEKS

Allium porrum

DIFFICULTY LEVEL: MEDIUM

The delicious, mildly oniony flavour of leeks has long been underestimated, relegated to comfort eating rather than haute cuisine. But whether cooked or chopped raw into salads, it's a useful vegetable that's ready to eat through the barren months of autumn and winter. The Welsh have long been leek-lovers – they even adopted it as one of their national emblems after winning a battle in a leek field against the Saxons in the seventh century.

SOWING

Leeks are space-hungry slow growers, so they're often started off in seedbeds until the first fast crops (such as lettuce) in the main vegetable plot have been harvested. Alternatively, you can plant them in their final positions and intercrop between the rows (see Intercropping, page 90) until they get bigger and need the space.

Prepare the seedbed by digging in plenty of compost the autumn before, then level it in spring and add a general fertiliser in March or April, a week before sowing outside. Make 13mm (½in) drills 15cm (6in) apart and sow thinly. When the seedlings appear, thin them to 3.5cm (1½in) apart. If you only need a few leeks, sow them in trays: one seed to a module, and leave them outside. Once the seeds have germinated, pot them on until they're ready to plant out to their final positions.

GROWING

When the leeks are pencil-thickness and about 20cm (8in) tall, they're ready to plant into their final positions. Water them well the day before transplanting and as you lift each one, trim off the tips of the roots and leaves. This will encourage the roots to branch and take up more nutrients, and reduces the moisture loss through the leaves.

To transplant, place the leeks into holes 15cm (6in) deep and 15cm (6in) apart in rows 30cm (12in) apart. Don't backfill with soil, just pour in water to settle the roots. Hoe regularly between the plants to keep the weeds down and water during dry periods. Once the leeks are more developed, you can begin to blanch the stems to increase the length of the white part. Do this by drawing up dry soil around the bottom of the leeks in stages until late October. Don't feed unless you want to increase the thickness of the stem, which looks good but doesn't improve the flavour.

COMPANION PLANTING

As part of the allium family, which includes garlic and onions, leeks repel many damaging insects and so are good companions to plants that are susceptible to infestation. With their upright growth they do not provide much shadow, which makes them useful for intercropping with fast-growing smaller crops, such as small lettuces, radishes and beetroot.

HARVESTING

Mini veg are always delicious, so start lifting the leeks, using a fork, while they are still small to prolong the harvesting period.

They can be left in the ground through the winter and be taken out of the ground when needed.

PROBLEMS

Onion white rot shows itself as wilted yellow leaves and a fluffy growth at the base of the leek. It can only be treated by disposing of any infected plants, and the spores can remain in the soil for a long time, so don't grow garlic, onions or leeks there for eight years.

Leek moth is a new problem mainly in the south east of England. Tunnelling caterpillars create whitish-brown patches on the leaves that turn yellow and rot. Infected plants should be destroyed. A covering of horticultural fleece in May and June will stop the adult moths laying eggs, and again between August to October. Adult moths and their pupae overwinter in plant debris, so be meticulous when clearing the plot.

ONION

Allium cepa

DIFFICULTY RATING: EASY

Onions are a culinary mainstay: a base ingredient for most soups, stews and savoury dishes. Quite apart from their usefulness in the kitchen, they are great companions in the vegetable patch. They emit an odour that repels many pest insects, so put them near plants that are prone to infestation. Added to that, they have obligingly upright leaves that don't overshadow other plants, so they make good companions for intercropping and catch crops (see page 90). Don't write onions off, even if you don't have space for a decent-sized bed; mini plantings of them throughout the patch (though nowhere near beans) could provide mutual benefit.

PLANTING

Onions and their smaller milder cousins, shallots, can be grown from seed or sets, which are immature bulbs, although growing from sets is a much faster and more reliable method.

Buy sets online or from garden centres that have been treated against viruses and heat-treated to stop the flower from forming. Plant the sets as soon as you buy them (any time between mid-March and mid-April), because you don't want shoots to appear before you get them into the ground. Some varieties are available as autumn-planting sets for an earlier crop, which will be ready to harvest in late spring and early summer. This is useful if you have a small plot with limited space in which to produce summer crops. Onions and shallots like good free-draining soil. Avoid freshly manured

ground, though, as this could rot the sets.

Prepare the sets by removing the papery skin at the top – this is so that they don't attract the attention of birds, which are very good at lifting newly planted sets. Shallots are the first to be planted, between mid-February and mid-March. Mark out rows 30cm (12in) apart and plant them 15cm (6in) apart. Gently push them into position so that the tip is just showing on the surface and firm in the soil around them.

Onions are planted in the same way between mid-March and mid-April, but placed 10cm (4in) apart. Mulch to conserve the soil moisture and keep down weeds.

GROWING

All you need to do is leave onions to get on with it. You need only water them if the weather is dry and occasionally feed them with a liquid fertiliser. If any flower spikes form, cut them off immediately because they will use all the goodness from the bulb and quickly shrink it. Having said that, they do produce wonderful showy purple pompom flowers and you might want one or two to develop simply for decorative appeal! Once the non-flowering bulbs have begun to swell, stop all watering and feeding and clear away any mulch or soil to expose the top of the bulb so it can fully develop.

HARVESTING

Once the leaves have turned yellow and have bent over, it's time to use a fork to gently lift the onions. Throw away any that are

not firm or are diseased, then lay the rest out in the sun to dry. In wet weather, dry them out in the greenhouse or shed. Onion gluts can be added to Tomato chutney (page 224), Aubergine and mustard pickle (page 226), Allotment chutney (page 230), Curried carrot chutney (page 233), Beetroot relish (page 234), Caballero salsa (page 237), Fennel relish (page 238) and Garcia's green sauce (page 241).

PROBLEMS

Like leeks and garlic, onions can be susceptible to **onion white rot** and leek rust. In wet weather, they are also susceptible to **onion downy mildew**, causing grey-green patches on the leaves, which should be removed and destroyed immediately.

PARSNIP

Pastinaca sativa

DIFFICULTY RATING: EASY

Delicious, sweet, roasted parsnips must be one of winter's favourite vegetables, yet they're little known in French kitchens, where they share the same name as turnips. That's probably because for centuries they were mainly used in Europe as animal fodder and weren't deemed suitable for kitchen use. They're a great potager crop because they can be sown directly into the soil, are easy to grow and can be left just where they are until you're ready to use them.

SOWING

Parsnips are happy in most soils, though over-rich soils can result in parsnip canker, so prepare the soil by digging it over deeply in the autumn, but don't add extra manure. The seedlings don't take too kindly to being transplanted, so sow them directly into their final growing positions in the ground in March or April. As the weather warms up, rake over the bed and add some general fertiliser, then prepare 1cm (½in) drills 30cm (12in) apart and cover them with cloches to warm up the soil. A week or so later, choose a dry still day for sowing, because parsnip seeds are very light and easily blown away. Plant three seeds every 15cm (6in) along the drills and cover with soil. Once the seedlings are about 2.5cm (1in) high, thin them to the strongest in each station.

GROWING

Unless you have great depths of enviably good soil, choose a shorter variety that is resistant to canker as it will be easier to grow. You shouldn't need to water the parsnips, unless there's a dry spell when you'll need to keep them moist to avoid them becoming woody and splitting. Weed by hand around the plants instead of hoeing, to avoid damaging the crowns. The parsnips will not be ready for harvesting for several months, and some will still be in the ground at eight months, so if space is an issue in your patch, plant radish and lettuce as catch crops between them.

HARVESTING

You can start to harvest from mid-autumn when the foliage begins to die back, by carefully lifting them with a garden fork to avoid damaging the roots. Parsnips are a brilliant winter crop as they can be left in the ground until you're ready to eat them, and as the stored starch is converted to sugar at around freezing point, parsnips left in the ground during a frost are usually the tastiest!

PROBLEMS

Parsnip canker, which starts as an orangey brown or purple rot at the top of the root, can be caused by over-rich soil, drought or damage to the crown, though some growers say planting them too early can cause the problem. Choose a resistant variety like 'Avon Resistor'.

Protect the crop from the larvae of low-flying **carrot fly** that tunnel into the root. Do this by putting up a 60cm (2ft) high barrier (higher than the female can fly) made of polythene, specialist mesh, such as Enviromesh, or thin horticultural fleece.

PEAS

Pisum sativum

DIFFICULTY RATING: MEDIUM

Fresh garden peas, cooked and eaten within an hour of harvesting, are sweet, succulent and nutritious. Blanch them within that hour and they'll be just as sweet, but after that the sugars start turning to starch and the flavour is never so good. It has to be said that growing peas successfully takes a bit of practice, but with careful planning, once you have the knowhow, you could be cropping juicy peas from May till October.

The varieties fall into first early varieties, second earlies and maincrops, which are further classified as round varieties and wrinkled varieties (which is how they look when they are dried). There are also mangetout and petit pois varieties, which are the sweetest and easiest to grow. All of these are cultivated in the same way but they each have different sowing and harvesting times, so check the instructions on the seed packet.

SOWING

Choose a sunny plot that has not had peas growing on it for at least two years and in the autumn before sowing dig in plenty of compost or manure. If you're planting early in the year, warm up the soil using a sheet of polythene or cloches, then dig planting trenches that are the height of the fully-grown plant apart (check the seed packet for recommended spacings). These trenches should be 15cm (6in) wide and 5cm (2in) deep. Put the peas into this trench about 7.5cm (3in) apart and cover with soil. Water and mulch.

GROWING

Peas need support. You can use pea sticks for the dwarf varieties, though larger varieties will need trellis or bamboo canes. Unless it's very dry, you won't need to water until the plant begins to flower and the pods start to swell.

HARVESTING

Peas can be harvested continuously from late June right up until September. They are ready to be picked once the pods have reached a decent size. If in doubt, pop one open and see how big the peas are inside. They are best eaten when young and sweet, if you let them get too big they will lose their flavour.

PROBLEMS

Everyone, it seems, loves those sweet-tasting peas: pigeons, mice and pea moth larvae. The best solution is to cover the plants as soon as they are planted, using a fine mesh insect-proof netting to stop the birds and insects from getting at them.

Pea moths only mate once in the season, so you can avoid damage from their larvae by sowing in March or June. If you do want to sow during the pea moth season, you could confuse the pests with a pheromone trap, which interferes with their mating instincts.

Powdery mildew is another problem and often a sign that the plants are under stress. Make sure they are planted into good soil and do not dry out.

POTATOES

Solanum tuberosum

DIFFICULTY RATING: EASY

It can be very satisfying to wander down into the garden on a summer's day and dig up your own-grown delicious potatoes to cook for lunch. If you don't have a large garden, you might prefer to choose an early variety, which takes up less space and matures quicker than the maincrops. These can also be harvested as you need them, whereas maincrop potatoes all need to be harvested at once and then stored.

PLANTING

If you have the space and enthusiasm, you can dine on home-grown potatoes all year round. Plant first early varieties in March for a June harvest, second earlies in April for a July and August harvest, and maincrops in April for harvesting from August until early October. They can be planted in a sunny spot in almost any soil where potatoes have not been grown within two years.

Prepare the site in the autumn by digging it over and incorporating well-rotted manure to improve the soil. Potatoes are grown from seed potatoes, which are about the size of a small hen's egg. You can get these off to a good start by 'chitting' them, which means encouraging them to send out shoots before you plant. This will give you a better harvest. You'll notice that one end of the potato has more eyes than the other; this is called the 'rose end'. Place the seed potatoes rose end up in egg boxes in a light position at about 10°C/50°F and leave them to sprout. When the shoots are about 2.5cm (1in) long, they are ready to plant.

Prepare the potato beds by digging trenches of about 10cm (4in) deep set about 60cm (24in) apart for earlies and 75cm (30in) for maincrops. Now place the potatoes rose end up in the trenches 30cm (12in) apart for earlies and 37.5cm (15in) apart for maincrops. Fill the trench with soil, lightly covering the potatoes so as not to damage the shoots.

GROWING

If there's still danger of frost by the time the first shoots break through the soil, rake a little soil over them for protection. Once the plants have grown about 23cm (9in), they'll need to be 'earthed up' (covered with a layer of earth) to stop any potatoes near the surface being exposed to light and turning green. This also helps to protect against potato blight. Another way of protecting the potatoes from sunlight is to mulch around the foliage with plastic sheeting, which has the added benefit of keeping the weeds down and conserving moisture, as well as dispensing with the need to earth up. Early crops will need plenty of water in dry periods, especially when the tubers are beginning to form.

CONTAINER GROWING

If you don't have enough space to give over to growing lots of potatoes, you could cultivate up to five on the patio in a dustbin or one in a container about 30cm (12in) deep and wide. Earlies are probably the easiest to grow in containers as they are smaller and mature quicker and you get a good few in a small space.

If the container doesn't have any holes in its base, make some using a power drill. Add a 5–10cm (2–4in) layer of crocks, then top them with 10cm (4in) of container compost and place the chitted seed potatoes on top, equally spaced apart. Cover these with another 10–20cm (4–8in) of container compost. You'll need to keep the container well watered, especially during dry periods. As the shoots appear, cover them with more container compost and continue to do this until the compost reaches about 5cm (2in) below the rim of the dustbin.

HARVESTING

Earlies are ready to harvest when the flowers open, usually between 10 and 12 weeks after planting. If they haven't flowered by then, feel around the roots to see how the potatoes are developing to decide whether or not they're ready to dig up. If they are ready, carefully

put a fork into the soil well away from the main stem and lift up the whole plant. Most of the potatoes will come up with the plant but you may need to rummage around in the soil below to dig up more tubers. Be careful when you do this so as not to spear them with the fork. If you've planted under plastic, simply peel the sheet away and the potatoes should be lying on the soil surface.

You can start harvesting the maincrop in the same way from August, as the foliage begins to yellow, but as the season progresses you'll want to save some potatoes for storage (see Harvesting and Storing, page 96).

PROBLEMS

Potato blight is a fungal infection that can be a problem in warm wet summers; the disease will rot leaves, stems and, ultimately, the tubers. There's little that can be done, except destroy the diseased plants, preferably by burning them, or burying them more than 45cm (18in) deep. Don't grow any more potatoes on the site for at least four years.

Potato blackleg is a bacterial disease that rots the base of the stem, yellowing it and rotting the tubers. The infected plants should be destroyed and not composted.

Slugs will also chomp into the potatoes – to control them, see page 54.

PURPLE SPROUTING BROCCOLI

Brassica oleracea (Italica Group)

DIFFICULTY RATING: MEDIUM

The idea of harvesting your own delicate new shoots to eat in the dead of winter sounds unbelievable, but that's what you'll get, from January onwards, if you grow purple sprouting broccoli. It's a great green crop to tide you over until the first spring cabbages are ready. The only drawback is that it takes its time: about 44 weeks from sowing to eating. It's worth the effort, though, as purple-sprouting broccoli is a cut-and-come-again crop, giving you fresh daily greens through the hungry months. Don't expect it to produce large heads like the vegetable we buy in the shops. Although this is (somewhat confusingly) sold as broccoli and comes from the same family, the bought version is actually calabrese.

SOWING

Sow into individual biodegradable pots under cover from March until April, or outdoors from April until early June into a well raked-out seedbed to a depth of 1cm (½in) in rows 15cm (6in) apart. Once the seedlings are big enough, thin them out to about 7.5cm (3in) apart. When they are about 7.5cm (3in) tall, they're ready for planting into their final position. Plant them in a bed that was prepared in autumn by being dug over and plenty of well-rotted compost being incorporated. Allow plenty of space for each plant so there's room for the branches to grow. Work on the basis of 30cm (12in) between each plant and 45cm (18in) between rows. If that's a bit space-hungry for your garden, plant quick-growing crops between the rows which will be long over before the broccoli needs to produce the side shoots in early spring.

GROWING

Mulch around the broccoli to conserve moisture and water during dry periods. Feed with liquid fertiliser every two weeks once the main head has been cropped to encourage side branches to develop. Broccoli is top heavy and shallow rooted, so give each plant some support by staking each plant and earthing up the main stalk.

COMPANION PLANTING

Strong-smelling plants will deter insects, so plant broccoli near onions, garlic or rosemary.

HARVESTING

This is a cut-and-come again crop, so once the main flower shoot, or spear, has formed, snap it off and then the plant will start to produce side shoots, which you can harvest over a period of two months.

PROBLEMS

Pigeons and **caterpillars** love the young plants, and the larvae of **cabbage root fly** attack the roots, so cover them with a fine insect netting to protect them from birds and insects.

RADISH

Raphanus sativus

DIFFICULTY RATING: EASY

Rosy red, round and easy peasy to grow, pretty little radishes are the go-to crop to grow with your children. They'll see the first shoots appear a week or so after the seeds have been put into the ground, and they could be eating them within the month! But for all their cute looks, the fiery flavour of radishes adds a kick to any summer salad and makes them a great crudité vegetable. There are many varieties that are not available in the supermarket, so these are well worth growing.

For the gardener, its speedy germination and growth makes radish a really useful crop. It can be used to mark the positions of slow-to germinate seeds, such as parsnips, and then pulled out once the parsnip shoots have appeared or, more profitably, be used to quickly produce a harvest from the land between larger slower-growing vegetables such as leeks and broccoli. Radishes don't like to dry out, so in high summer you could even plant a few in the dappled shade of another crop, such as tomatoes.

SOWING

Seeds can be planted directly into the ground outside in February in soil that has been warmed up, then covered by cloches, or between March and mid-August and left uncovered. They are big enough to plant singly, though if you buy the pelleted versions they'll be even easier to handle. For fresh radishes all summer, you'll need to sow every two weeks, so it may be worthwhile investing in a seed dispenser so you can really zip down the rows.

The seeds should be put into ground that was dug and manured in the autumn (or, if you are planting in early spring, add some general fertiliser now). Make drills 1cm (½in) deep and 15cm (6in) apart and plant the seeds 2.5cm (1in) apart. Cover with soil.

GROWING

Keep radishes moist: if the soil is allowed to dry out, they will become woody and unpalatable. For this reason, it's easier to grow radishes in early summer than in July and August when everything has become rather dryer. If you don't have any kind of irrigation in place (see page 52), position them in the shade of other plants when sowing in high summer.

HARVESTING

Pull up the radishes while they are still young and succulent, as and when you need them.

PROBLEMS

Slugs and **snails** are partial to young radishes, so keep these pests under control (see page 54).

RHUBARB

Rheum x hybridum

DIFFICULTY RATING: EASY

Pretty, pink and slightly acid in taste, rhubarb makes a delicious dessert ingredient or accompaniment to some meats – and it also makes a striking statement in the garden. Although we eat it as a fruit, cooked with sugar, technically it is a vegetable, because the edible part is the stem. A hardy perennial, the rose-coloured stems appear each spring, supporting huge glossy green leaves. This is not a crop you'll be harvesting in a hurry, though. For the first year after planting, you need to let the plant settle in, put on some growth and build its strength. By the second year, you'll be able to take a few stems, then more in subsequent years. Traditionally, rhubarb was forced under tall terracotta forcing pots in early spring to make the plant produce paler pink stems that are sweeter than those grown open to the elements.

PLANTING

Few people would bother with growing rhubarb from seed; most people buy dormant crowns in the winter, ready for spring planting. Choose a sunny open site with free-draining soil that has been dug over in the autumn and had plenty of rotted manure forked in. Plant the crowns in March and prepare the soil by raking in a layer of general fertiliser. Dig a hole deep enough to accommodate the crown of the plant, with the top just visible on the surface, then gently prise the roots apart and position each plant 90cm (36in) apart. Rhubarb also grows well in large containers at least 50cm (20in) deep and wide.

GROWING

Rhubarb should be kept well watered whenever conditions are dry. Remove the leaves as they die back in the autumn to prevent the crown rotting in a wet winter and to expose it to frost, as this encourages a more abundant crop of stalks in the spring. Mulch around the crown in spring to preserve moisture, but do not cover it or it will rot.

HARVESTING

If you want to force your rhubarb plant, as soon as you see any shoots (around January) you'll need to exclude them from all light. You can either use a traditional terracotta rhubarb forcer, or an old chimney pot with the top covered up. Cover the stalks but check the growth, and when they reach the top, which should be in around six weeks, they are ready to harvest. Don't force the plant two years running – it will need at least a year to recover, so grow two or more plants so you can force them on alternate years.

To harvest rhubarb, whether forced or not, just pull the stalks out, giving them a gentle twist and avoiding snapping them. You can harvest stalks from plants that haven't been forced from April, but never denude the plant and always make sure there are at least four stalks remaining. Don't harvest any stalks after July.

Gluts can be frozen, or used in Redbarb cordial (page 220).

PROBLEMS

Rhubarb is relatively trouble-free, but it is occasionally attacked by **crown rot** or **honey fungus**. As these are both fungal diseases, the only cure for both is to dig out and burn the crowns. Do not plant rhubarb in the area for five years.

ROCKET

Eruca sativa

DIFFICULTY RATING: EASY

Delicious, peppery rocket is a favourite cut-and-come-again leaf that perks up any salad, aiding digestion and adding fibre, iron, calcium and vitamins A and C to your diet. Also known in Europe as roquette, rucola and rugula, and arugula in the United States, the English call it rocket because of the speed at which it bolts and goes to seed when the weather gets warm, sunny and dry.

SOWING

One or two rocket plants should be enough for any family because it needs to be picked regularly to keep the leaves coming. Sow two or three groups of seeds, about 1cm (½in) deep, straight into the soil from March. Once they come up, thin to the strongest plant at each station. Do this every two to three weeks until late August and you'll have delicious fresh salad leaves all summer. Alternatively, you can grow rocket in containers on the patio.

If you do want to grow rocket on a bigger scale, choose a sunny site with rich, well-drained soil and mark out drills 1cm (½in) deep and 25cm (10in) apart. Sow the seeds thinly and when the seedlings are large enough to handle, thin them to 20–30cm (10–12in) apart.

GROWING

Keep the bed weed-free and the plants moist. Don't overwater as this can reduce the strength of the peppery taste, but don't let them get too dry either otherwise they'll bolt in no time.

HARVESTING

You'll be able to start picking the leaves four weeks after sowing. Pick a few from each plant, rather than denude one, which will weaken it. Pinch off any flower buds as soon as you see them, otherwise the plant will put its energies into bolting, forming flowers, and seeds and the flavour will soon go out of the leaves.

PROBLEMS

Bolting is a problem. Keeping the plants moist helps, as does putting them in partial shade – which is one of the advantages of growing them in containers, as you can move them out of trouble on blisteringly sunny days.

If **flea beetles** become a problem, pick them off and cover the plants with horticultural fleece.

SALAD LEAVES

Lactuca sativa

DIFFICULTY RATING: EASY

Lettuces and salads are summer favourites that are quick and easy to grow. You can start picking salad leaves just four weeks after sowing and lettuce after twelve weeks. Getting a good harvest isn't the problem: keeping up can be. Lettuces enthusiastically just keep on coming, maturing all at the same time and you can be pushed to cut and eat before they bolt. One solution is to sow short rows every two weeks. If one or two lettuces bolt, you can leave them to distract slugs and snails from the rest of the crop. There are endless varieties of lettuce, but most fall within one of the three groups: butterhead, which have an open habit; cos, which have longer, upright leaves; and crispheads, which have dense hearts and are less likely to bolt.

SOWING

Lettuce seeds can be sown directly in the ground from March until August. Choose a sunny or semi-shaded plot. If you didn't dig manure into the plot last autumn, dig in some a month before planting, or use container compost. Rake the soil to a fine tilth, then sow the seeds thinly at a depth of 1cm (½in) in drills 30cm (12in) apart. Cover the drills with a fine fleece to protect the seeds (and young seedlings) from birds and insects. For a regular supply, sow a short row of seeds every few weeks. Lettuce seeds don't germinate in hot weather, so in high summer, sow in the evening and water with icy water.

GROWING

Keep lettuces well watered – don't let the ground dry out as this causes the lettuces to bolt. You can plant them in the shade of larger plants, such as courgettes. As soon as the first true leaves appear, start to thin out, and thin again later until they are 30cm (12in) apart.

HARVESTING

Cut the lettuces just below their lowest leaves using a knife. Butterheads need prompt harvesting as they bolt readily. Crispheads can be left standing longer, otherwise the plant will put its energies into forming flowers, bolting and seeds and the flavour will soon go out of the leaves.

PROBLEMS

Slugs and snails (see page 54). Birds love seedlings, so cover with fleece or bird netting. **Grey mould** can appear on mature plants, especially in cold damp summers. Make sure the lettuces have plenty of ventilation. If you spot mould, destroy the lettuces. **Lettuce root aphid** can attack roots in dry summers; you can see their work when the lettuce dies back. Ease the problem by keeping the lettuces well watered. Pull up and destroy affected plants.

SPINACH

Spinacia oleracea

DIFFICULTY RATING: EASY

Delicious fresh young spinach leaves, packed with nutrition and antioxidants, add flavour, texture and colour to any salad, making this a valuable cut-and-come-again crop. The leaves can also be steamed or boiled lightly, though you might want to wait until the plant is more mature and the leaves larger, as they reduce in size dramatically when cooked. If you plant both summer and winter varieties, you'll be able to harvest spinach for most of the year, bar a few weeks in early summer.

SOWING

Spinach grows best in a rich soil, so dig in plenty of well-rotted compost before planting and adding in some general fertiliser. Summer varieties can be sown every few weeks straight into the ground from mid-March until the end of May. Winter varieties can be sown in August and September.

Sow the seed thinly in drills 2.5cm (1in) deep and 30cm (12in) apart. Spinach does not like to dry out, so sow later summer crops under the shade of taller leafy crops. It will also grow happily in a large container.

GROWING

When the seedlings are big enough to grasp, thin them out so they are 7.5cm (3in) apart. After a few more weeks, pull out every other plant and allow the remaining ones to grow – you can use the thinnings in salads. Keep the plants well watered during dry spells, otherwise the spinach can bolt and the leaves become bitter. If you are growing winter spinach in a particularly frost-prone area, it might be worth covering the plants with horticultural fleece or cloches from late October/early November until all risk of frost has passed.

HARVESTING

Start picking the leaves as soon as they are large enough to eat, carefully cutting them off with secateurs, or pinching them off with your fingernails to avoid damaging the plant. In the summer, you can take up to half the leaves with no ill effects on the plant, and the more you pick, the more they'll produce. Be more sparing with the amount of leaves you take from winter varieties.

PROBLEMS

Spinach downy mildew might attack the plants in wet weather. Choose a mildew-resistant variety and keep the plants well spaced so air can circulate well around them.

If birds start helping themselves, protect the plants with fine netting.

Spinach is more likely to bolt in very hot, dry weather, so keep it well-watered or plant it in light shade under larger plants.

SWEETCORN

Zea mays

DIFFICULTY RATING: MEDIUM

Delicious freshly cooked sweetcorn dripping with butter has been a summertime treat for generations. A traditional American saying exhorts people to walk slowly to pick it and run home to cook it. They might not have known why, but they knew that the quicker they cooked it after harvesting, the better it tasted. This is because once picked, the sugar in the kernels quickly converts to starch, thereby affecting the taste, so the quicker you cook it, the sweeter it is. However it is not an efficient use of a small space – every row will give you only one cob per 30cm (12in). But you can factor in more than just the cobs. Sweetcorn, along with runner beans and squash, is one of the legendary Three Sisters (see page 113).

SOWING

Sweetcorn is a bit of a fussy starter; the seeds take their time to germinate and don't take too kindly to root disturbance. However, you can speed up the germination process to get the plants off the starting blocks. Lay a layer of well-spaced kernels on soaked kitchen paper in a baking tray, then put another layer of soaked kitchen paper on top. Water lightly, put the whole thing in a loosely tied plastic bag and leave in a warm place until the kernels swell and tiny roots begin to form. Do this between mid-April and early May.

Next, prepare for as little root disturbance as possible. Carefully plant each seed in its own biodegradable 7.5cm (3in) plant pot filled with compost. Start more seeds than you need to allow for any that don't make it. Once the seedlings are established and the frosts are over, harden them off ready for planting out.

GROWING

Sweetcorn likes well-drained soil in a sunny position, ideally in soil that is slightly on the acid side. Dig over the bed in autumn and dig in plenty of compost for good moisture retention. Prepare the bed just before planting by raking in a general slow-release fertiliser. The seedlings need to be planted in rectangular blocks and not in single rows in order to offer the best possible conditions for wind pollination. Plant the seedlings in the ground, biodegradable pot and all, so they are 45cm (18in) apart in both directions. Keep growing on spare seedlings in their pots to replace any planted in the block that don't survive.

Mulch to keep the bed moist and weed-free. Hoeing can be a problem as the roots of sweetcorn often appear above the soil and should not be damaged, so protect them by earthing up. Also, don't cut off any side shoots, which are known as tillers. Keep the plants watered in dry weather, especially when flowering. In late June or July, when the tassels are fully developed, gently tap them to release the pollen and encourage fertilisation. Give the plants a liquid feed to help the kernels develop.

HARVESTING

The cobs will be ready for harvest when the silks have turned

chocolate brown and started to wither. Check ripeness by pulling back some leaves and squeezing a couple of kernels with your fingernails. If the liquid that runs out is clear and watery, they're not quite ready, but if it is milky in colour and texture, they are ready to cut.

PROBLEMS

Large galls, known as **smut balls**, can appear on the plant in hot and dry weather. If allowed to mature, these can burst open, releasing black spores and infecting the surrounding plants. The galls must be cut off as soon as they appear and burnt. If any plants are infected by smut, all the plants should be burnt after harvest and sweetcorn should not be grown on the site for at least three years.

TOMATOES

Lycopersicon esculentum

DIFFICULTY RATING: EASY

There's nothing more delicious than a sun-ripened tomato picked and eaten straight from the vine, especially if it's in your own garden! Said to reduce the risk of cancer and heart disease, tomatoes are also claimed to be anti-inflammatory and high in antioxidants, and have been a staple in the healthy traditional Mediterranean diet for centuries. They are wonderfully satisfying to grow and, for the space they take up, they produce a generous harvest, of about 2kg (4lb) per plant. Native to South America, tomatoes are happiest in warm sunny climates, but given a sheltered suntrap there are several varieties that will grow happily outside in southern Britain and make a satisfying beginner crop.

VARIETIES

Tomatoes can range from marble-small (cherry tomatoes), to huge beefsteak varieties. The medium-sized tomatoes (round or plum) are probably the best for beginners: cherry tomatoes can be fun, but the harvest isn't usually so rewarding and the larger beefsteak tomatoes can sometimes break their vines. Size aside, tomatoes fall into two main types: **Cordon**, or indeterminate, varieties produce fruiting trusses straight off the main stem. You need to pinch out the side shoots as they appear, otherwise the plant will divert some of its energy into producing tomatoes on these too and you're likely to end up with a lot of green tomatoes around the time of the first frosts. For the same reason, when the fourth flower truss has appeared,

pinch out the lead growing tip to stop the plant from continuing to grow upwards. **Dwarf, or bush** varieties don't grow any higher than 75cm (30in) high, and do not need pinching out or staking. These are a good choice for beginner gardeners and for container growing on the patio or balcony.

SOWING

The easiest way to grow tomatoes is to plant bought seedlings straight out into the ground in around late May. This is not difficult if you live in a mild area of Britain and the summer is sunny rather than very wet; however, tomatoes won't do well in the colder parts of Britain. If you have any doubts, check out the local garden centre; they will only stock varieties that are suited to your area's growing conditions and climate. Choose healthy-looking dark green plants about 20cm (8in) tall, and check the base of the containers to make sure they are not potbound.

If you do have a greenhouse, you'll have a much wider choice of varieties if you buy from seed. Sow these in seed compost in February or March either in seed trays or plant two seeds in each cell of a modular tray. If you want only a few plants, sow two or three seeds each into 7.5cm (3in) biodegradable pots that you can later pot on without disturbing the roots. Keep them moist but not over-wet. Once the seedlings have established, prick out the tray-grown ones, or pull out weaker ones from the modular cells or biodegradable pots, leaving only

the strongest seedling in each. When they reach about 20cm (8in) and the first flowers appear, it's time to get them outside.

GROWING

Greenhouse-grown plants need to be planted out into growbags or large pots filled with multipurpose compost. Tomatoes are self-pollinating, but you can give them a nudge by leaving the greenhouse doors open to invite in insects, tapping the canes, misting with water up through the plant, or distributing the pollen using a small paintbrush.

If you're growing outside, your seedlings will be ready to go out at the end of May after a period of hardening off (see page 44). Choose a warm, sheltered, sunny spot, such as against a south-facing wall, and plant them in soil that was dug over and had plenty of well-rotted compost forked in the previous autumn.

RUNNER BEANS

Phaseolus coccineus Papilionaceae
DIFFICULTY RATING: EASY

A week before planting, rake in some general fertiliser. Plant the seedlings 45cm (18in) apart in rows 75cm (30in) apart. Water the plants well. Dig a hole slightly larger than the pot and put a layer of multipurpose compost in the bottom. Gently remove the plant from the pot, place it in the hole and fill around it with multipurpose compost. Water in. If you are growing a cordon variety, push in a stake, being careful not to damage the roots, and tie the seedling in loosely using soft garden string. Bush varieties do not need staking. Keep the bed weed-free and water regularly to keep the ground moist without over-wetting it. Tomatoes grown in growbags or containers need regular, balanced watering: if you alternate allowing them to dry out then flooding them with water, you risk splitting the developing fruit.

If you are growing a cordon variety, you'll need to pinch out the side shoots. The reason for this is to encourage the plant to produce good-sized fruits up the main stem that ripen before the frosts. You'll see these side shoots appear between the leaf stem and the main steam, so just remove them using your fingernails, leaving the leaf in position. Remove any leaves as they yellow below the fruit trusses. As the tomato plant grows, tie it in to the stake every 30cm (12in). Don't overwater or overfertilise the plants as this is often the cause of many tomato problems. However, once the fruits are beginning to form, you could feed with tomato fertiliser following the manufacturer's instructions. If the tomatoes are taking their time to ripen, cut off any yellowing leaves covering the fruits so they can soak up every drop of sunshine.

COMPANION PLANTING

French marigolds deter whitefly and tomatoes are said to be helped by alliums, nasturtiums, borage and oregano being planted nearby. One study claims that tomato harvests can be improved by 20 per cent if basil is grown alongside the plants. Be that as it may, it won't do any harm, and having the tomatoes and basil close to each other is very handy when it comes to gathering together ingredients for a delicious summer salad.

HARVESTING

Bush-type tomatoes should be ready to harvest eight weeks after they were planted, cordon types about twelve – just break them off at the joint above the fruit. If frosts threaten towards the end of the season and the fruits are still green, cover bush varieties with a cloche or horticultural fleece at night or move them indoors if they are in pots. Cordon tomatoes can be uprooted and hung upside down in the greenhouse or shed to ripen, or they can be cut and stored in a paper bag with a ripe banana, which is rich in ethylene that encourages the tomatoes to ripen. Alternatively, or if they refuse to ripen, green tomatoes can be cooked up into a green chutney (see page 224). Ripe tomatoes can be preserved in Tomato chutney (page 224), Caballero salsa (page 237) or as Drowned tomaotes (page 252), or used to add colour to floral arrangements – see Topiary tree, page 200, and Summer table arrrangement, page 195.

PROBLEMS

The range of potential problems associated with growing tomatoes can be off-putting, but many arise because of the way in which the plant is cared for, rather than because of pests and diseases.

Blossom end rot shows in dark patches at the ends of the tomatoes and is the result of inappropriate watering. To avoid this, water regularly, rather than sporadically, and do not let the soil dry out. Remove any rotten tomatoes, adjust the watering and new fruits should not be affected.

Tomato blight, which is a fungal disease that rots fruit and foliage, is most common if there has been persistent wet weather. Your best approach is to choose resistant varieties, but if it is a very wet summer, try to rig up a waterproof shelter. If the blight appears, destroy the plants by pulling them up, putting them in plastic bags and disposing of them in the local recycling centre. Do not put them onto the compost heap, otherwise the blight could reappear next year.

Split fruits are usually due to erratic watering. Water regularly to keep the soil moist. **Yellowing leaves and stems** are sometimes caused by over feeding. However tempting it is to spoil those plants, don't kill them with kindness. Hold back on the fertiliser if you've been over enthusiastic with it and follow the manufacturer's instructions.

BASIL

Ocimum basilicum

DIFFICULTY RATING: MEDIUM

A native of India, sweet basil is a most delicious, peppery-flavoured herb that is used generously in Mediterranean and Thai dishes. It is a tender annual that won't survive frosts but is happy when grown in a warm sunny position in the garden. It grows well alongside tomatoes, and one study showed that when in this position the tomato yield can increase by up to 20 per cent. Nobody's quite sure why, it may simply be because they both like warm sunny positions and with both crops in the same place, you'll make more visits and remember to water them!

It's easiest to save yourself the hassle of sowing and buy young plants in garden centres, but if you prefer to start from scratch you can sow seeds indoors between January and April or outdoors from May. The leaves are ready to harvest about six weeks after sowing. Basil will thrive in a large pot, which is a sensible arrangement because it can be taken under cover if there is a prolonged wet period which might encourage fungal diseases.

Basil can be harvested by pinching off shoots. If you do this regularly, you not only benefit the salads but you also stop the plant producing flowers and going to seed, which robs the leaves of their flavour.

BAY

Laurus nobilis

DIFFICULTY RATING: EASY

This elegant relation of laurel has wonderfully aromatic, robust leaves which are used to infuse sauces as well as add flavour to dishes through casseroling, boiling, poaching and sautéeing.

An evergreen shrub or small tree, bay is not difficult to grow; in fact it can reach 7.5m (23ft) high. It's easiest bought as a small plant, to be dug into a sheltered spot. If you want to limit its growth, plant it in a container filled with a compost such as John Innes No3 mixed with some controlled-release fertiliser granules. Grown this way, do not let the soil in the container dry out.

Pot-grown bay can be clipped into topiary shapes. When grown in the ground, young trees can be pruned lightly in the spring or summer. Once mature, they can be hard-pruned. Bay is pretty hardy and can generally tolerate cold temperatures, but if it is in a container, wrap the pot in bubble wrap or fleece if the temperature threatens to drop below freezing.

CHIVES

Allium schoenoprasum

DIFFICULTY RATING: EASY

A member of the onion family, the grass-like leaves of chives are used to gently flavour salads and soups.

Chives are perennial, so will return year on year with the right care. You can grow them from seed, but plants are widely available. Snip the leaves to within 2.5cm (1in) of the ground as you need them and don't strip the plant bare of leaves if you want them to return next summer.

The perky purple-pink flowers are a delight, and many people use them for colour in a herb garden, planted 10cm (4in) apart as a border. If you want to retain the flavour, stop them from flowering by cutting the plants to within 2.5cm (1in) of the ground halfway through summer to encourage more leaves. Don't cut them down after August; you need to let the sun reach their leaves until they naturally die down, to replenish the bulb ready for next year's growth.

CORIANDER

Coriandrum sativum

DIFFICULTY RATING: MEDIUM

DILL

Anethum graveolens

DIFFICULTY RATING: EASY

The distinctive, aromatic flavour of coriander makes it a popular herb in Indian, Thai and other Eastern dishes. The seeds are also used, stir-fried whole or ground (see Blueberry curd, page 219; Aubergine and mustard pickle, page 226; Quickalilli, page 229, Curried carrot chutney, page 233; Caballero salsa, page 237; Preserved courgettes, page 251).

Happiest in a warm sunny climate, coriander is not easy to grow in northern climes. Sow the seed in a sunny position from late spring, after the frosts, until autumn. Sow thinly, directly into its final growing position, as coriander does not like to be moved. Once the seedlings are large enough to handle, thin out to 5cm (2in) apart. Alternatively, buy plants at the garden centre. Coriander can flop about, so support it and harvest regularly to prevent it going to seed. Once you can detect the lemony smell of the ripening seed, cut the flower stems and dry the seeds (see page 88).

This pretty annual umbellifer with its feathery foliage is sometimes confused with its close family member, the perennial fennel. As herbs they are very similar in taste, and both have seeds that are used as spices. Some say they should not be grown near to each other because they can cross-pollinate and create a foul-tasting herb. Although others refute this theory, it may be best to grow one or the other.

Standing at around 60cm (2ft), dill is shorter than fennel, which can grow to a height of 1.5m (5ft). Dill seeds should be sown in April in a sunny well-drained spot that has been raked to a fine tilth. When the seedlings appear, thin them out to 30cm (12in) apart. Once the plant is big enough, you can snip off leaves as you need them to delicately flavour fish dishes. At the end of the season, either leave the plant to self-seed for next year, gather and dry the seed (see page 88), or use to preserve other crops, such as courgettes (see page 251).

FENNEL

Foeniculum vulgare

DIFFICULTY RATING: MEDIUM

This hardy perennial is sometimes confused with annual dill (see opposite). Quite apart from being a delicate aromatic herb, the bulb-like root of some varieties of fennel can be grown as a vegetable, the seeds can be harvested as a spice or the leaves used in cooking – see page 238 for Fennel relish. The elegant, feathery leaves also make it a decorative border plant.

The easiest way to grow fennel is to buy young plants and plant them from April in a sunny position in fertile, moist and well-drained soil. Cut the leaves to use for flavouring when you need them. If you'd like to collect the seed, use the same method described on page 88. Although fennel is perennial, it's an enthusiastic self-seeder, so if you want to keep it under control, cut down the flowers before they turn to seed.

LEMON BALM

Melissa officinalis

DIFFICULTY RATING: EASY

Lemon balm has a delicate lemony flavour that can be used to enhance fish dishes and salads.

An uncomplaining bushy perennial that grows to about 1m (3ft) high, lemon balm loves rich moist soil in a sunny position, but will perform almost anywhere. Lemon balm can be invasive, so if space is at a premium and you don't want it taking over, grow it in a container or plant it in a pot sunk into the ground.

LEMON VERBENA

Aloysia triphylla

DIFFICULTY RATING: DIFFICULT

Native to Chile, lemon verbena has the strongest flavour of all the lemony herbs.

In contrast to the robust lemon balm, lemon verbena is a tender shrub that needs a sunny position protected from frost. If you are growing it in the north of the country, it is worth offering the plant protection or bringing it indoors over winter. Growing up to 3m (10ft) high, lemon verbena should be planted in light, free-draining soil, and if frost threatens it should be protected with a layer of mulch around the roots. If the plant does suffer over winter, nurture it with gentle pruning and spraying with warm water in the spring. Don't give up on it quickly, it can sometimes be well into the summer before the new shoots appear.

MINT

Mentha

DIFFICULTY RATING: EASY

The main problem you're likely to have with mint is to stop it growing. Once it gets going, it can be very invasive, so either grow it in a container on its own or plant it in a pot and sink it into the ground. Alternatively, you could lift the plant at the end of the season and divide and replant just a part of the root.

Don't grow mint near another mint, as they tend to lose flavour. Growing so abundantly, you can use mint with abandon! Its delicious fresh flavour can be used to perk up drinks, desserts and savoury dishes, or can be used to make Mint jelly (see page 246), a traditional accompaniment to roast lamb.

OREGANO

Origanum vulgare

DIFFICULTY RATING: EASY

Translated from the Greek, oregano means 'joy of the mountain' – and little wonder, as this pretty hardy perennial blankets its native Mediterranean mountains in heady aromatic green leaves and tiny purple flowers. The same horticultural name '*origanum*' is used for what the Greeks call oregano and the British call wild marjoram, though the plants have evolved differently; oregano being more aromatic than the delicate marjoram.

These are invaluable herbs that can be used as substitutes for basil and parsley, though they are much easier to grow. In southern Britain origanum doesn't even die down in milder winters. Buy a pot-grown plant and plant it in the ground. You can pinch off the leaves as you need them, and in a couple of years it will provide attractive ground cover in the herb bed or in the flower borders. Golden oregano, *Origanum vulgare* 'Aureum', is particularly attractive.

PARSLEY

Petroselinum

DIFFICULTY RATING: MEDIUM

A favourite herb used in traditional English cooking, there are two types of parsley: curly leafed and the stronger-flavoured flat leafed. As well as adding flavour to salads, casseroles, stews and preserves (Fennel relish, page 238), parsley counteracts the smell of garlic on the breath. Parsley is not easy to germinate, so it's better to buy ready-grown plants.

Although parsley is a hardy biennial, it quickly goes to seed in the second year, so should be dug up as soon as the next year's plants are ready for use. To harvest parsley year round, grow plants in two separate positions: some for summer harvesting in light shade and some in a sheltered sunny spot for winter use. Parsley needs good rich soil, so dig in plenty of compost or well-rotted manure the autumn before planting. In summer, keep the plants moist. For the best flavour, remove any flower buds as they appear.

ROSEMARY

Rosmarinus officinalis

DIFFICULTY RATING: EASY

Rosemary is a frost-hardy evergreen shrub with aromatic needle-like leaves that can be used to flavour roast meats and stews throughout the year, and can also be used to perk up preserved gluts, such as Drowned tomatoes (page 252).

This Mediterranean herb will be happiest in a south-west-facing sunny position in well-drained soil. Plant it as a young plant into its final growing position. In the spring, rosemary produces pretty purplish blue or white flowers, and so can make a pretty addition to the border. Rosemary can become unruly; so once it's finished blooming, prune it back into shape.

SAGE

Salvia

DIFFICULTY RATING: EASY

The pungent, almost medicinal, flavour of sage perfectly complements meat and is often used in stuffing.

The classic sage, *S. officinalis*, is the best variety from a culinary point of view. It is also an attractive evergreen with pretty silvery blue-green leaves that look good in the border. Sage also comes in purple and gold varieties. Although hardy enough to survive most winters, it's a good idea to cover it with horticultural fleece in its first year, or if it's a particularly cold year.

Sage should be pruned back in the spring to encourage young shoots as well as the pretty mauve flowers. Over time, sage becomes woody, so you might want to uproot the plants after about four years and start again.

THYME

Thymus

DIFFICULTY RATING: EASY

If you only grow one herb, let it be thyme. This undemanding, low-growing, aromatic evergreen shrub will give you fresh herbs all year round in return for very little effort that can be used in a multitude of dishes, including Drowned tomatoes (page 252).

Thyme loves droughts and is happy growing in poor soil, though choose a well-drained, sheltered position, especially if you live in a wet climate, and perhaps add a gravel or grit mulch to keep the leaves from resting on wet soil. If you live in a very cold area, you could simply grow it as an annual, re-planting every year.

The easiest way to cultivate thyme is to buy young pre-grown plants. There are endless varieties available: silver-leaved, golden-leaved, variegated, each carrying flowers in shades ranging from white and palest pink to deep purple.

FRUIT

APPLES

Malus domestica

DIFFICULTY RATING: EASY

In terms of productivity, apple trees are hard to beat. A mature garden tree will give you around 100 fruit a year, while apple farmers can harvest up to 300!

There are over 5000 named varieties, yet very few appear in supermarkets, so it's worth buying a tasty unusual variety from a specialist grower. Buy in containers or as bare-root plants (which are cheaper) in winter.

Even the smallest plot can have an apple tree; they are grafted onto rootstocks (the root of another tree), which determine the eventual size of the tree. Sometimes the rootstock is of a completely different fruit. Depending on the rootstock, you can choose from trees that will eventually grow to 2.5m (15ft) down to 1.2m (4ft), or even dwarfs that can be grown in pots.

As well as standard trees, specialist growers also supply young trees that they've trained as fans, espaliers or cordons to be grown against walls. A more modern option is a columnar tree (also called minarette), where all the fruiting spurs grow off the central trunk (see page 144).

PLANTING

Ideally, apple trees should be planted during their dormant period – between early December and the middle of March. Choose a suitable sunny site with well-drained soil that is clear of other tree roots and buildings. Many varieties need another apple tree to assist in pollination, so if you have space, plant another to complement it, or look around, as often there is one nearby.

Dig the soil thoroughly and remove any weeds. When you're ready to plant, water the tree well. Dig a large hole 1m (3ft) square and 45cm (18in) deep. Now loosen, but don't remove, the subsoil and mix in well-rotted manure or garden compost. Place the root ball in the hole with the top of the compost from the pot level with the ground and backfill using the soil you have just excavated. Firm down the soil and water well. Using a sledgehammer, drive in a 2m (6ft) high by 5cm (2in) diameter stake on the side of the prevailing wind, then tie in the tree loosely using a rubber tree tie.

GROWING

Water the tree well during its first season with 10–15 litres (2 gallons) or two full watering cans of water every week, unless it rains heavily. Mulch and keep the area weed-free. Apply a general fertiliser over the roots in February and June.

PRUNING

Unless you have a trained tree (page 144), pruning is straightforward, simply remove dead, damaged and diseased branches in the winter while the trees are dormant.

HARVESTING

Fruits will begin to ripen from August into September, depending on the variety. Pick as they ripen, and make sure all are harvested by October before winter winds set in. Delicious in puddings or jams (Blackberry and apple jam, page 216; Bramley apple and chilli jelly, page 245; Mint jelly,

page 246), or as juice or a cordial (Apple and ginger cordial, page 222). Cookers are great as savoury chutneys: Green tomato (page 224) or Allotment (page 230).

PROBLEMS

Generally, apple trees don't present many problems. However, **codling moths** can munch their way through fruits. Set up pheromone traps over the summer to lure in and destroy the males before they mate. **Aphids**, which damage young leaves, can be kept in check by ladybirds. If you spot the fluffy, waxy secretions of woolly aphids early in the year, scrub them off using a stiff-bristled brush. **Powdery mildew** can affect flower buds and the tips of young shoots and these should be sprayed with fungicide as they appear. **Scab** leaves unsightly marks on fruit and foliage, and **canker** can cause bark to shrink and crack. Affected parts should be removed and burned.

Trained tree types

Specialist fruit tree growers can supply young trees that have been trained over their first few years into various shapes to be grown against walls or as boundaries. The foundations have been 'laid', but you will need to continue to prune and train them to develop and maintain that shape. Established suppliers should provide instructions as to how to do this when you buy the tree.

ESPALIER TREES

Grown against a wall, these have a central trunk with side branches trained along horizontal wires.

FAN

This is similar to espalier, but the branches fan out from lower down the trunk, rather than growing out horizontally (top right), and are tied in to wires fixed to the wall in a fan shape. This technique is mostly used for plums and cherries.

CORDON

Where space is limited you can grow a cordon, which is a line of trees set at a 45-degree angle and trained along wires. The horizontal wires should be fixed at 60, 120 and 180cm (2, 4 and 6ft), and the trees planted at spacings of 60cm (2ft).

COLUMNAR, MINARETTES AND BALLERINA

These are similar to cordons but are grown vertically, rather than at an angle.

STEP-OVER

These are (usually apple) trees where the two branches running horizontally along wires 45cm (18in) high above the ground so you can literally step over the plant (right). They are ideal for plots where space is limited, as they make a delightful edging to a vegetable bed and give you a miniature apple orchard into the bargain!

BLACKBERRIES

Rubus fruticosus
DIFFICULTY RATING: EASY

Sweet sun-ripened blackberries bursting with flavour must be one of early autumn's best treats. They are delicious on their own, comforting made into a jam (see Blackberry and apple jam, page 216) and fabulous made into a pie with their autumn teammate, the apple, but ask any gardener and most will say they would rather NOT grow them. They would far rather gather ripe blackberries from the hedgerows than let a single blackberry plant venture through the garden gate. The reason is that they are viciously thorny, speedy growers, stubbornly rooted and pretty invasive. However, some new cultivars have been developed that are rather easier to control, and there are even some thornless varieties available, such as 'Loch Ness'.

PLANTING

Give a blackberry a sunny, sheltered site and it will thrive and thank you with a bountiful harvest. Give it a slightly shaded site and it will survive but perhaps not be so generous with its fruits. Blackberries should be planted against a wall or fence at least 1.5m (10ft) high with horizontal wires fixed to it, spaced 45cm (18in) apart – the lowest one being 23cm (9in) above the ground. If you don't have a boundary, attach horizontal wires to two wooden posts and grow the blackberries along them. Plant the blackberry in a deep hole of well-drained soil, and allow for a covering of about 8cm (3in) of soil. Once it is planted, cut the canes down to one healthy-looking bud to encourage the plant to throw up more canes.

GROWING

Young plants will need watering every seven to ten days during dry spells, but other than that the blackberries will grow with alacrity with very little help from you: keeping them under control is likely to be the greater challenge.

PRUNING

At the end of the first autumn, cut back all the side shoots to 5cm (2in) lengths to encourage fruiting spurs to develop. In spring new canes will appear from ground level, which should be tied into the supports. When the old canes have finished fruiting later in the season, cut them down, then train the new canes along the wires. Cut the tips off the new canes in late summer to ensure they don't grow down and root themselves into the ground.

HARVESTING

Harvest the blackberries as soon as they are fully ripe – which is from around midsummer onwards. They are best eaten fresh but gluts can be easily frozen or used in preserves.

BLACKCURRANTS

Ribes nigrum

DIFFICULTY RATING: MEDIUM

The sharp flavour of these delightful shiny berries is wonderful in jams (see Blackcurrant jam, page 216), jellies and tarts, although traditionally vitamin-packed blackcurrants were most popularly used medicinally for coughs and colds. Blackcurrants are often grouped together with red- and whitecurrants when it comes to discussing growing methods, but blackcurrants have different pruning needs because they fruit on new, not old, wood.

PLANTING

Blackcurrants can be grown in the ground or in a container of at least 45cm (18in) diameter. If you're planting in the ground, choose a sunny spot and prepare the ground a few weeks before by digging in plenty of well-rotted manure and some general fertiliser. Just before planting, water the plant and let it drain – the idea is to thoroughly wet the rootball before putting it in the ground. Pull up any weeds on the site, then dig a hole at least twice the size of the rootball so that the top of the compost around it will lie 7.5cm (3in) below the ground level. Place the plant in the hole, spreading out the roots to encourage new shoots to grow from the base. Pack John Innes No3 around the rootball, filling the hole and firming it in, then water well.

If you're planting in a container, start with a layer of crock at the bottom to aid drainage, and use two-thirds John Innes No3 to one-third grit. You'll need to re-pot every two to three years;

simply remove the plant from the container, trim back the roots a little and re-pot either in the same or a slightly larger container using fresh compost.

PRUNING

Prune blackcurrants in the winter while they're dormant by cutting back old wood to leave fruit-forming young shoots. For the first four years, any weak shoots should be removed to leave the plant with between six and ten strong shoots. By the time it is five years old, you should take out one-third of the older wood from the base.

HARVESTING

Pick blackcurrants once they turn shiny black, cutting off the strigs if all on it are ripe, or removing individual fruits if some are not yet ripe.

PROBLEMS

Blackcurrants can be prone to **fungal diseases**, **big bud mite** and **blackcurrant gall midge**. To avoid these, buy certified resistant varieties, but check exactly what they are resistant to as it may be only to some but not all of these diseases. If in doubt, choose a variety, such as 'Ben Hope', which claims to be resistant to big bud mite, which is the most difficult problem to deal with.

Big bud mites are a gardener's headache because they infect the buds in the winter before they have opened, so there is little you can do other than pick off and destroy infested buds. If the plant becomes heavily infested,

you must uproot it and destroy it, preferably by burning.

Gall midge is a lesser problem in that you'll be able to see tiny white maggots that feed on the shoots and the young leaves shrivel and die. Pick off any infected leaves and destroy them. If you do this early on and don't have to remove too many shoots, the plant should still yield a reasonable harvest.

Avoid fungal diseases by not planting the blackcurrants too closely together so there's good ventilation, pruning out old wood and not allowing the plant to dry out in periods of drought.

Birds will keep their beady eyes on the fruits and, given half a chance, they'll zoom in to decimate the harvest. Cover the plant with fruit nets to keep them at bay (see also page 86).

BLUEBERRIES & BILBERRIES

Vaccinium

DIFFICULTY RATING: MEDIUM

Picking and eating delicious indigo bilberries straight off their low-growing bushes was a traditional summer delight for northern European children playing in coniferous forests or heaths nearby. This was a crop that was collected, rather than cultivated, and in Finland, Germany and Scotland these berries were particularly popular, where they were made into tarts, jellies and country wines, or simply eaten fresh with a little milk. Northern American blueberries are the bilberries' near relative. They grow on bushes, which are much easier to pick from, although some, such as the Highbush, do grow up to 4m (15ft) high. Most, however, are crossed varieties and usually grow to a more manageable knee height.

Now considered a nutritional superfood, blueberries have become a popular soft fruit that is ready early in the summer. However, this is not one you can even consider growing in the ground unless you have an acid soil (see page 30) with a pH value of 5.5 or lower. If you don't have acid soil (which is generally a good, rather than bad thing) you can grow blueberries in a container filled with ericaceous compost (see page 40).

PLANTING

Blueberries produce a much better harvest if they are grown near another plant of a different cultivar, so aim to grow at least two. Most are a deep indigo colour, but you can also get almost raspberry-coloured versions, and the combination could make a

pretty display. Each plant will need to be started off in a container of at least 30cm (12in) diameter, but will eventually be potted on to one of up to 50cm (20in).

You MUST use ericaceous compost in the pots, which is available from garden suppliers. Thoroughly water the plants a few hours before transplanting and allow them to drain. Meanwhile, place a layer of crocks in the bottom of the container, followed by a layer of ericaceous compost. Try it out for depth by putting the potted blueberry plant into the new container. The compost level should come to about 3cm (1½in) below the lip of the new container. Now carefully tip the plant out of its old container, being careful not to damage the roots, and put it centrally into the new container. Pack more ericaceous compost around the edges, pressing it in with your fingers, and then add a 1cm (½in) layer to the top. Water it again and put it into position – they will tolerate shade but you will get a better crop in full sun.

GROWING

Keep the compost moist, using rainwater if possible as tap water will raise the pH level of the soil. Feed them every month using a liquid fertiliser specially formulated for ericaceous plants. After two years, in late February or early March, prune out as much of the old wood as possible, without damaging the plant, to encourage new fruit-bearing growth.

HARVESTING

Once the berries change from green to their characteristic indigo or red, which should be around midsummer, you can start to harvest. Revisit the plant regularly as the berries don't all ripen at once. If you have a glut, try making Blueberry curd (page 219).

PROBLEMS

Given half a chance, **birds** will get the berries before you do, so use bird scarers or protect the plants with nets (see page 86). Also, **aphids** like to attack the berries, so squish any you see between your fingers as soon as you spot them, or draft in some ladybirds (see page 77) to keep them under control. **Powdery mildew** can be another problem if the plants become stressed in dry conditions.

CHERRIES

Prunus avium

DIFFICULTY RATING: MEDIUM

Cherry blossom is one of spring's most stunning gifts to the countryside and a wonderful addition to any garden, even without the reward of the delicious summer fruits.

A member of the plum family, cherry trees are available as sweet dessert cherries or sour cherries, such as Morello. Just one mature tree can produce up to 60kg (130lb) of cherries in a year! You don't have to just grow them as a traditional tree – if you have a wall or put up some horizontal wires attached to posts you could train the trees as fans, espaliers or cordons (see page 144).

PLANTING

Cherry trees should ideally be planted while dormant – any time between early December and mid-March. Choose a sunny site with deep, well-drained soil. Choose a warm sheltered site or a south-facing wall where the trees can be protected from winter frost, which could damage the blossom. Many varieties need another cherry tree to assist in pollination, so choose a variety that is self-fertile and does not need a pollinating partner. Ask the nursery for advice.

Dig over the soil thoroughly and remove all the perennial weeds. When you're ready to plant, water the tree well. Dig a large hole 1m (3ft) square and 45cm (18in) deep. Now loosen, but don't remove, the subsoil and mix in well-rotted manure or garden compost. Place the rootball in the hole with the top of the compost from the pot level with the ground and backfill using the soil you have just excavated. Firm down

the soil and water well. Using a sledgehammer, drive in a 2m (6ft) high by 5cm (2in) diameter stake on the side of the prevailing wind, then tie in the tree loosely using a rubber tree tie.

GROWING

Water the tree well during its first season with 10–15 litres (2 gallons) or two full watering cans of water every week, unless it rains heavily. Mulch and keep the area weed-free. Apply a general fertiliser over the roots in February and June. When blossom appears and frost is forecast, protect the tender buds with horticultural fleece overnight. Be sure to remove the fleece in the morning to allow pollinating insects access to the flowers.

PRUNING

Avoid pruning cherry trees to keep silver leaf disease at bay. If you are

growing a trained variety, prune in spring as new growth appears and again in late September.

HARVESTING

Leave the fruits on the trees until fully ripe. If the birds are getting to the harvest before you, cover the branches with nets.

PROBLEMS

Birds are a real problem but can be held at bay by nettting.
Blackfly will be tempted by the young shoots in spring; the clusters of these pests should be wiped off with a damp cloth.
Canker can affect trees and damaged stems should be removed and disposed off.
Silver leaf can be another problem (see also Plums, page 151). Try to catch this disease early; remove affected parts, and avoid pruning in autumn and winter when the spores are released.

GOOSEBERRIES

Ribes uva crispa

DIFFICULTY RATING: MEDIUM

Freshly picked sun-ripened gooseberries explode with flavour in your mouth and are ample reward for very little input. The plant itself is a rather untidy bush which stands 1.5m (5ft) high, though they can be bought as cordons to grow against a wall, or as a standard with a tall trunk and neat ball head. Gooseberries can also be grown in containers.

PLANTING

Choose a plant that is at least two years old with three to five main branches and clear stems 10–15cm (4–6in) long. These will need to be planted 1.2–1.5m (4–5ft) apart. If you want to grow them against a wall, buy bushes that have been trained as cordons (see page 144). They will be around 40cm (18in) tall, and should be planted 45–60cm (18–24in) apart. Plant any time between late autumn and early spring when there are no frosts. Choose a well-ventilated or even breezy site, with rich soil and plenty of compost dug in. Mulch to conserve moisture. Cordons planted at the base of walls may need additional watering.

GROWING

Gooseberries in the ground should not need watering unless there is a prolonged dry spell. Keep the compost moist in container-grown plants. Add some general fertiliser in winter, though don't overdo it, as it could encourage mildew.

PRUNING

Gooseberries should be pruned between November and the end of January as they will not fruit on wood that is older than four years. The aim is to produce a goblet-shaped bush with an open centre so there is plenty of ventilation. You also want to aim for upward-growing stems. Start by pruning out the old wood down as low as you can. Next, cut out any branches that cross or touch each other, checking the inside of the bush carefully, and cut away any low branches so that they are well clear of the ground.

HARVESTING

Ripe gooseberries will be ready to pick from mid July. You can also pick under-ripe ones to bake into tarts and pies.

PROBLEMS

Birds can be a problem, though they're no more partial to stabbing themselves on the vicious thorns than we are, so they will plunder other fruit first if it's more readily available. If the birds do start tucking into the gooseberries, cover the bush with fruit netting. **Mildew** is another problem, which is best tackled by buying a mildew-resistant cultivar, siting the plant in a well-ventilated or breezy position and pruning it into an open goblet shape. If mildew appears, cut off and destroy any affected branches. **Gooseberry sawfly** overwinters in the soil as a cocoon and the adults emerge in April to lay torpedo-shaped eggs on the undersides of leaves, usually in the middle of the bush. The hatched larvae will chomp away in the middle of the bush for a couple of

weeks and then work outwards, continuing to chomp for three more weeks before dropping to the ground to pupate. If you don't catch them early, you could have three or four generations sharing the bushes in one season. In early April, check the undersides of leaves, especially any that have 'pinholes' in the centre of the bush and remove any leaves with eggs or larvae on them. This is much easier to do if you have cordons, which are more open than the bushes. If you don't spot them until they have moved outwards on the bush, it might be too late. The best plan of action then, is to spray the bush with pyrethrum or thiacloprid-based spray. If you are gardening organically, there is a nematode (*Steinernema carpocapsae*) that will deal with them. In the autumn and winter, remove mulches from around the roots to encourage birds to forage for the overwintering sawfly pupae.

PEARS

Pyrus communis

DIFFICULTY RATING: EASY

Very like apple trees, pears obligingly produce abundant harvests in return for very little effort. When mature the trees are considerably larger than apples, naturally growing to 3–6m (10–20ft), which is out of proportion for many urban gardens, and certainly far too lofty for convenient harvesting.

For this reason they are often grafted onto the rootstock of shorter-growing quince, or even hawthorn. Some pears have been grafted onto rootstocks, which means they can be grown in containers, happily fruiting, even if they're hard-pruned to keep their dwarf size and shape.

You don't have to just grow them as traditional trees – if you have a wall or put up some horizontal wires attached to posts you could train them as fans, espaliers, cordons or even a step-over (see page 144), or choose a more modern option, such as a pole-like columnar tree (also called minarette), where all the fruiting spurs grow off the central trunk.

PLANTING

Pear trees are best planted during their dormant period – between early December and mid-March. Choose a suitable sunny or dappled site with well-drained soil, and because pears produce blossom early in the year, choose a sheltered position to protect them from frosts, which could damage the flowers. In cooler climates, pears are happiest planted near south-facing walls.

Dig over the soil thoroughly and remove all the perennial

weeds. When you're ready to plant, water the tree well. Dig a large hole 1m (3ft) square and 45cm (18in) deep. Now loosen, but don't remove, the subsoil and mix in well-rotted manure or garden compost. Place the root ball in the hole with the top of the compost from the pot level with the ground and backfill using the soil you have just excavated. Firm down the soil and water well. Using a sledgehammer, drive in a 2m (6ft) high by 5cm (2in) diameter stake on the side of the prevailing wind, then tie in the tree loosely using a rubber tree tie.

GROWING

Water the tree well during its first season with 10–15 litres (2 gallons) or two full watering cans of water every week, unless it rains heavily. Mulch and keep the area weed-free. Apply a general fertiliser over the roots in February and June.

PRUNING

Unless you have a trained tree (see page 144), pruning is easy, simply remove dead, damaged and diseased branches while the trees are dormant (between late October and March).

HARVESTING

Fruits begin to ripen from September, depending on the variety. Pick as they ripen; they may change colour or your clue may be the drop of windfalls.

PROBLEMS

Birds are a real problem but can be held at bay by nettting.
Blackfly will be tempted by young shoots in spring; wipe off clusters of pests with a damp cloth.
Scab can leave unsightly marks on fruit and foliage; all affected parts should be removed and disposed of.

PLUMS

Prunus domestica
DIFFICULTY RATING: EASY

The variety of these English garden favourites seems endless, from the traditional and popular Victoria plum to all the damsons, greengages and mireilles, which makes these trees some of the most popular grown in gardens. The trees produce an abundant crop, so much so that you may need to thin the fruit during the growing season to give them room to develop.

Many plum trees, and other members of the family, need a partner to assist them in pollination, so you may need to buy a second tree if there isn't another in a neighbouring garden.

PLANTING

Ideally, plum trees should be planted during their dormant period – any time between early December and the middle of March. Choose a warm sheltered site or a south-facing wall where the trees can be protected from winter frosts which could damage their blossom. Dig over the soil thoroughly and remove all the perennial weeds. When you're ready to plant, water the tree well. Dig a large hole 1m (3ft) square and 45cm (18in) deep. Now loosen, but don't remove, the subsoil and mix in well-rotted manure or garden compost. Place the root ball in the hole with the top of the compost from the pot level with the ground and backfill using the soil you have just excavated. Firm down the soil and water well. Using a sledgehammer, drive in a 2m (6ft) high by 5cm (2in) diameter stake on the side of the prevailing wind, then tie in the tree loosely using a rubber tree tie.

GROWING

Water the tree well during its first season with 10–15 litres (2 gallons) or two full watering cans of water every week, unless it rains heavily. Mulch and keep the area weed-free. Apply a general fertiliser over the roots in February and June. Plum trees should be pruned in summer, around June, not in autumn, as they can be prone to silver leaf disease, the spores of which are most prevalent in autumn and winter. Remove new growth that is not bearing fruit and pinch out this year's new side shoots to six leaves from the parent branch to encourage fruit the next year. When the main stem reaches about 2.5m (8ft) high, prune it back to about 1m (3ft) above the highest branch.

PRUNING

Avoid pruning plum trees to keep silver leaf disease at bay. If you are growing a trained variety, prune in spring as new growth appears and again in late September.

HARVESTING

Leave the fruits on the trees until fully ripe – between late July and September. If the birds are getting to the harvest before you, cover the branches with nets.

PROBLEMS

Birds are a real problem but can be held at bay by nettting. Wasps also love plums, so set traps around the trees or leave them the windfalls to feast on.

Silver leaf can also affect trees. Try to catch this disease early and remove affected parts, and avoid pruning trees in autumn and winter when the spores are released.

RASPBERRIES

Rubus idaeus

DIFFICULTY RATING: EASY

Always delicious, raspberries are something of a superfood, packed with fibre, antioxidants, which are thought to help resist cancer, and vitamin K, which increases bone-mineral density. If you plant both summer-fruiting and autumn-fruiting varieties, you could be harvesting from late August right the way through to October with very little effort. Their upright canes are happiest grown against a wall or boundary, and because they take up very little space, they can be grown even in the smallest plot.

PLANTING

The dormant season, between November and March, is the best time to plant. Choose a sheltered sunny position with fertile, slightly acidic soil. Raspberries are traditionally planted against a wall, fence, or on wires between posts, but you can train a plant up one post or grow one in a container if you have limited space. Plant when the ground is not frozen or waterlogged; start by clearing the site of perennial weeds, then plant the canes 45–60cm (1½–2ft) apart, in rows 1.8m (6ft) apart. Finally, mulch with bark or coconut husk to suppress weeds (don't be tempted to mulch with manure, as this is too rich and may burn the developing shoots), then prune the canes to within 25cm (10in) off the ground. Container-grown raspberries should be potted up one to a 38cm (15in) pot filled with a 50:50 mix of John Innes No3 and multipurpose compost, then trained up bamboo canes.

GROWING

Keep raspberries watered in dry periods, particularly if they are against a wall or in a container where the rain won't always reach. In mid-spring, sprinkle a general-purpose fertiliser around the roots, then mulch to stop weeds taking hold. In summer, pull up suckers that appear between summer raspberries and thin the autumn canes to 10cm (4in) apart.

PRUNING

Once the harvest is over, cut back all the canes that fruited to the ground. Tie in 6–8 of the strongest young canes, 8–10cm (3–4in) apart, along the wire supports, then cut off the remaining stems at ground level. All autumn-fruiting raspberry canes should be cut down to ground level in February.

HARVESTING

Pick the berries when firm and juicy and a deep red. Pull them off gently, if the fruit does not come away cleanly it is not quite ripe. They freeze well, or are delicious in Raspberry Jam (page 214).

PROBLEMS

Weak or stressed raspberries canes are susceptible to fungal diseases such as **raspberry cane blight, raspberry spur blight** and **raspberry cane spot**. Keep plants well ventilated, mulched and watered. Cut off and dispose of any affected parts. **Raspberry beetle larvae** can be seen inside the raspberry when you pick it; there is no preventative measure. The traditional treatment is to spray with insecticide, or a non-chemical alternative is to spray with an organic horticultural soap or oil. Prevent birds sharing the crops, by covering with netting.

REDCURRANTS AND WHITECURRANTS

Ribes sativum

DIFFICULTY RATING: MEDIUM

Shiny bright redcurrants explode in your mouth with a refreshing, slightly tart flavour, making them one of summer's treats. Whitecurrants are simply (often slightly sweeter) albino varieties of redcurrants. Although they're often grouped together with blackcurrants, they differ in that they fruit on old wood, rather than new. Redcurrants are available as bushes, which are pretty when in fruit but are not spectacular and are fairly space-hungry – you'll need to allow 1.75m (5ft) between bushes. If you don't have a large garden, you may prefer to grow them as cordons against a wall, or as a standard with a trunk-like stem topped with a rounded head, reaching 1.75m (5ft) high, which makes a pretty, decorative feature in the garden.

PLANTING

Red- and whitecurrants produce their sweetest harvests when planted in a sunny, sheltered site, but they'll also fruit in partial shade or when planted against a north-facing wall. They don't demand as rich a soil as blackcurrants, and prefer it to be neutral to acidic. Prepare and plant them as blackcurrants (see page 146), but place them so the top of the soil they were potted in is at ground level. Finish with a mulch of well-rotted compost.

If space is an issue, they can also be container-grown. Choose a cordon or standard currant to grow in a pot, water it well and let it drain. Place a layer of crocks in a 45cm (18in) container, followed by a layer of multipurpose compost

or John Innes No3. Place the plant in the container, then fill around it with compost, pressing it in firmly with your fingers, and water well. Keep container-grown plants well watered at all times, and fertilised every fortnight from late winter to early spring. Stand containers on feet for good drainage, to stop the roots from rotting over winter. Every three years, remove them from the pot, shake off as much compost as possible, trim the roots by one-third and repot into a slightly larger pot with fresh compost.

GROWING

Water newly-planted bushes during dry weather. Mature bushes should not need watering except during long periods of drought. Top-dress plants with a general fertiliser in February.

PRUNING

Redcurrants bear fruit on old wood, so pruning should be done in early summer. Aim to create an open goblet shape to encourage good ventilation, which protects against fungal diseases. Start by cutting out old or diseased wood (this part can also be done in winter), then cut new growth back to two buds. Prune the main branches to outward-facing buds to encourage the goblet shape, or, if they are bending downwards, prune to an upward-facing bud.

Cordons should be pruned in early spring. Cut any new growth on the main stem by a quarter of the previous year's growth, unless the new stem is weak, in which case you can cut back up to half

of it. Try to keep a balanced shape when pruning. When the main stem has reached the optimum height, prune it back to one bud of new growth each year in early summer and cut back the sideshoots to one bud to increase fruiting.

HARVESTING

Pick the berries when they're firm and juicy and the redcurrants are a bright red. It is easiest to cut off whole strigs rather than try to pick individual berries. Lovely in puddings or lend a jewel-like colour to cordials such as Redbarb or Curranty cordial, page 220.

PROBLEMS

Red- and whitecurrants are prone to **gooseberry sawfly** (see gooseberries, page 149). **Birds** would like to share the harvest, so net the bushes.

STRAWBERRIES

Fragaria

DIFFICULTY RATING: EASY

Juicy red strawberries are at their delicious best when picked fully ripe in the middle of a sunny day and eaten immediately. They are the iconic summer fruit and remarkably easy to grow! They're happy growing in their natural position, on the ground, but you can also grow them in containers and even in hanging baskets.

Strawberry plants are available ready-to-plant in the spring from garden centres, or, if you're organised enough, you can buy plant runners (shoots, sent out by the strawberry plant, complete with a mini 'daughter' plant) in the autumn.

PLANTING

Prepare a bed for the strawberries in a sunny but sheltered spot in the autumn by digging in plenty of compost or well-rotted manure, then plant out either in autumn or spring. The plants should be spaced 45cm (18in) apart in rows 75cm (30in) apart. Water the plants well first and let them drain. Dig individual holes each deep enough to accommodate a plant with the top of the pot's compost level with the soil surface. Fill the hole with multipurpose compost and firm it in well. Finally, water in.

If you're planting runners, spread out the roots and make sure the crown of the plant is resting at soil level. Put a strawberry mat around each plant to keep the weeds down, protect the plants from slug damage and to keep the strawberries off the soil when they appear. Copper-coated mats are great because they send out an electric charge that keeps the slugs well clear.

Container-grown strawberries should be planted three plants to a 30cm (12in) pot or basket. Plant them in container compost and add water-retaining gel and slow-release fertiliser granules.

GROWING

Once strawberry plants start to flower, feed with a high-potash liquid fertiliser every week or two weeks. Cut off any runners (daughter plants) that appear over the growing season as these will compete for nutrients with the flowers and fruits. Growing the strawberries under a tunnel cloche will bring forward the harvest by a week or so. If you are not growing your plants on matting, tuck straw under the developing fruits to lift them off the soil and prevent rotting.

After all the strawberries have been harvested, keep the bed well weeded and cut away any dead foliage, as this can harbour pests and diseases. Dig up the strawberry plants after three years as they will be past their best by then. If you'd like to continue growing strawberries, plant them in a new bed.

HARVESTING

Strawberries should be harvested in the middle of sunny days when their flavour is at its best. If you have lots of strawberries at the end of the summer, you can preserve them to have a flavour of summer when the season is over. Try making Petalberry Jam (page 213) or Curranty coridal (page 220).

PROBLEMS

Cover the strawberry patch with netting to stop the **birds** getting the fruit first.

Fungal diseases are sometimes a problem. Cut away any fruit that shows any sign of mould and keep the bed clear of any rotting leaves.

FLOWERS

AGAPANTHUS

Agapanthus Half-hardy perennial
DIFFICULTY RATING: MEDIUM

PLANT CLASSIFICATION:

Annuals complete their lifecycle in one year: germinate, grow, flower, set seed and die.

Biennials live for two years. They put on most of the growth in the first year, die down and then flower and seed-set in the second year.

Perennials are herbaceous plants that do not have woody stems. They die down in winter and re-appear the next spring. As their root system develops year on year, they'll often put on more leafy growth each summer as they mature.

Shrubs are woody plants that have several branches growing from their base, rather than a trunk. They can be evergreen or deciduous.

Bulbs, tubers, corms and rhizomes are all underground adapted stems or leaves that are the plants' storage systems. These plants die down in the winter and regenerate in the spring.

Hardiness ratings:
Hardy plants can withstand the cold to -20°C (-4°F).
Half-hardy plants will die if exposed to temperatures below -5°C (23°F).

This beautiful, statuesque plant, with its lush emerald-green strappy leaves and generous blue, purple, pink or white orbs, looks a bit like a giant allium and grows to over 1m (3ft) tall. Agapanthus looks fabulous in simple modern gardens as well as in a classic herbaceous border and containers. *Agapanthus africanus* is an evergreen that originates from South Africa, and though the blue variety can withstand a light frost, it is much more tender than its deciduous cousins, which die down in autumn and cope better with cold winters. These hardy varieties tend to be smaller, although there are three large perennials that survived the harsh London winter of 2009–10 unprotected: *A.* 'Northern Star', *A. inapertus* 'Midnight Cascade' and *A.* Headbourne hybrids. In particularly cold parts of the country, though, best results may be achieved by growing these plants in a cool conservatory.

Blooming from midsummer to early autumn, agapanthus brings colour to the garden even through the flower-famine month of August. Each plant produces a good show of flowers. The flowers turn into spectacular sputnik-like seedheads in autumn, which are also good for flower arranging. Leave a few on the plant for show, and to let them self-seed, which they do surprisingly readily if the conditions are right.

GROWING

Choose a sunny spot and plant agapanthus in moisture-retentive fertile soil, positioning the crowns 5cm (2in) below the soil surface.

Alternatively, plant in a pot 20–23cm (8–9in) diameter, using multipurpose compost. Keep the container weed-free. Agapanthus is fairly drought resistant, but does appreciate extra water during dry periods. In the winter, mulch the crowns for protection. If a very cold snap threatens, protect the pot with a fleece and zip the plant into a fleece jacket. In spring, pull out any dead or dying leaves. Don't be too hasty to re-pot agapanthus: they flower best when their roots are constricted. Every four to six years, divide the crowns – either in the autumn when they have finished flowering, or in spring before the buds have formed.

CUTTING & CONDITIONING

Cut agapanthus stems when the florets are still tightly closed so that they have a long vase life. Snip off the individual florets as they fade and die to extend the life of the others.

CARNATIONS AND PINKS

Dianthus Perennial, biennial and annual

DIFFICULTY RATING: EASY

Pretty pink, red or white carnations, with their long, almost grass-like grey-green leaves. They are a favourite cut flower, loved by florists because they're long lasting and have slim, pliable stems that are useful for arrangements. They are part of the dianthus family, which includes pinks, the dainty little-sister of the more blousy carnations.

Carnations and pinks fall into several groups: these are the main garden types:

Border carnations can be evergreen or annual, have sturdy stems and produce just one flush of up to five semi-double or double flowers on each stem in high summer. You can either leave all these to bloom or, if you want fewer larger specimens, pinch out all the lower buds, leaving just the leading bud to flower. They may need staking if the blooms become large and heavy.

Perpetual-flowering carnations are evergreen perennials that are grown commercially as cut flowers under glass. Outside, they will flower all through the summer, producing a regular supply of fully double flowers up to 10cm (4in) across. To achieve this size, just the terminal (leading) bud should be allowed to bloom; all the rest should be pinched out (disbudded) as soon as they appear.

Old-fashioned pinks are frost-hardy evergreens and smaller than carnations. Their sweetly scented single or double flowers are just 3.5–6cm (1½–2in) across, giving them a delightful cottage-garden appeal.

Modern pinks are a cross between old-fashioned pinks and perpetual-flowering carnations, and so will produce two or three flushes of blooms throughout the summer. Cut them regularly to keep the flowers coming!

GROWING

Carnations will happily grow in any well-drained soil in a sunny spot. Keep the bed free from weeds to reduce competition and do not let the soil dry out.

CUTTING & CONDITIONING

Using a sharp pair of secateurs, cut the stems to length just above a node (where the stem bulges) at a 45-degree angle. This will help them to draw up more water so that they sit nicely in the vase.

CATMINT

Nepeta Hardy perennial
DIFFICULTY RATING: EASY

Catmint might not be a classic cut flower, but it is an abundant all-summer standby for the florist. Producing a succession of pretty lavender-like flowers from late spring right through to autumn, catmint provides the flower arranger with months of material. Choose one of the larger varieties of catmint, such as *N.* 'Six Hills Giant', or *N. racemosa* 'Superba'.

GROWING

Catmint can be grown as a single clump or as a pretty hedge-like border in almost any soil, so long as it's in a sunny site. It's easy to grow from plugs, which is an inexpensive option if you want to plant a border.

Cut and deadhead the flowers regularly to encourage later flushes. The flowers and leaves will die down in the autumn, exposing woody stems. Leave these in position to protect the crowns over winter, and in the spring, when the shoots start to appear, just cut away the dead stems.

CUTTING & CONDITIONING

Cut the flowers either in the morning before the sun gets hot, or in the evening. Before arranging, strip off the leaves which grow below the blue flowers.

CHRYSANTHEMUMS

Chrysanthemum Perennial, annual
DIFFICULTY RATING: MEDIUM

Chrysanthemums are one of the top hobby flowers to grow and cut because they come in myriad forms and a range of colours in the pink/orange/red/yellow end of the spectrum plus creams and white. They offer a wide variety of long-lasting flowers on good sturdy stems for the arranger (see Summer Wreath, page 196; Hanging floral design, page 199) and plenty of challenges for the grower in terms of knowledge and skills. Little wonder the chrysanthemum has become a popular candidate for prizes at the village show!

Although most garden chrysanthemums are perennial, they usually don't survive the winter in northern Europe, except in particularly mild areas, so in autumn you should cut down half-hardy or frost-tender varieties, carefully dig them up and overwinter them in pots indoors.

GROWING

Chrysanthemums need to be planted as rooted cuttings or plugs, both of which are available from mid-March by mail order. If you don't have anywhere to grow them under cover, wait until May in milder parts of the country or June in colder areas before ordering. That way, you should be able to plant them outside without fear of damage by frost.

The plugs should be planted in a sunny site in well-drained soil that has had plenty of well-rotted compost dug in the previous autumn. Thoroughly water them, then plant them 20cm (8in) apart and water in. Drive in a bamboo cane to a depth of about 45cm

(18in) as support for the plant as it grows. Larger, container-grown chrysanthemums can be planted outside if they are suitable for growing outdoors and not intended for life in the greenhouse or conservatory.

Keep the chrysanthemum bed well weeded and watered. To encourage strong bushy growth you'll need to 'pinch out' the growing tip once it's reached about 20cm (8in). If you want a single showy bloom, keep the growing tip but remove the sideshoots and buds. This has to be carefully timed if you're growing to show, so that the flower arrives at its blooming best on the day.

In the autumn, when the flowers have gone over, cut the plant down and overwinter it planted upright in a tray of compost under cover. As soon as you see signs of life in the spring, start watering.

CUTTING & CONDITIONING

Use sharp secateurs to cut the stems to length at a 45-degree angle and strip off any leaves that will lie beneath the water line in a vase before arranging the chrysanthemums. Pick off any dead or limp leaves daily and recondition the stems every other day by cutting off another 5cm (2in) from the stem, washing them clean of any slime, and replacing them in fresh water. Given this treatment, they could last a fortnight or longer.

FLOWER TYPES

The variety of chrysanthemum flowers available is giddying,

which is part of their fascination, because there are always more to discover. They fall into several types:

Incurved petals originate from the base of the flower, curving upwards towards the crown to create a dense spherical flower.

Reflexed flowers have curved pointed petals that grow from the crown down towards the stem.

Intermediates are doubles with loosely incurving petals.

Single flowers have about five rows of petals growing at right angles to the stem and have a gold centre.

Pompons are double, dense and spherical with tubular petals that grow outwards from the crown.

Spoon-types look like singles, but they have tubular petals that open out at the tip to make a spoon shape.

Spider forms have long, thin, ray florets with petals that curve downwards to give a spider-like look.

CORNFLOWER

Centaurea cyanus Annual

DIFFICULTY RATING: EASY

COSMOS

Cosmos Half-hardy annual

DIFFICULTY RATING: EASY

Cornflowers are native to northern Europe, and their joyous bright blue flowers can be seen blooming wild in fields and hedgerows all through the summer from June to September. Although cornflowers have now been cultivated in pinks, reds, purples and white, none of these shades quite matches the charm of the original blue.

GROWING

Cornflowers are incredibly easy to grow: just choose a well-drained site and sprinkle some seed from April to July in prepared garden soil, and with a bit of deadheading they'll reward you with flowers from June to November.

CUTTING & CONDITIONING

Cut the stems with sharp secateurs and strip off any leaves that will sit below the water line in the vase.

There's a sweet innocence to cosmos; nothing showy or blousy, just pretty, single, daisy-like flowers in a joyous range of pinks, plums, yellows, oranges and even chocolate. They dance up to 1m (3ft) high above a froth of feathery leaves and, like chorus girls, they just keep the show going all summer. For the price of a packet of seed and very little effort, you'll be able to pick their flowers from July right up until the end of September, with plenty left behind to keep the garden pretty.

GROWING

Native to Mexico, cosmos doesn't like the cold, so you can't just scatter the seed in the ground as you would native hardy annuals. The seeds need a temperature of 18–25°C (64–77°F) to germinate, so they should be started off under cover in March or April. Keep the soil damp and you should

see signs of life within 7–15 days. When the seedlings are large enough to handle, transplant them into 7cm (3in) individual pots and let them continue to grow until all chance of frost is over, then harden them off (see page 42) ready for planting in their final positions outside. Choose a sunny site and plant them 45cm (18in) apart. Pinch out the growing tips to encourage them to branch out and produce more flowers. Keep the soil moist and weed-free. Keep picking to encourage more growth and deadhead any blooms that go over, cutting them off at the first leaves.

CUTTING & CONDITIONING

Use sharp scissors to cut the flowers and strip off the lower leaves. Leave them plunged in a bucket of water for an hour or two to give them a good drink before arranging.

DAHLIA

Dahlia Perennials (mostly half-hardy)
DIFFICULTY RATING: DIFFICULT

By August, most summer flowers are over and the garden is, frankly, past its lush best. Then along come razzle-dazzle dahlias with their exuberant hues to cheer the borders and provide enough blooms to cut and take inside right up to the first frosts. Given the right conditions, a single plant can produce up to 100 flowers at this otherwise barren time of year.

Available in many single, double and decorative forms, there are more than 1500 varieties to choose from, all in the red/yellow/orange spectrum. On the downside, dahlia tubers can't survive the frost, so you'll need to dig them up and store them under cover over winter. The plants are also prone to quite a few pests and diseases. They're worth the challenge, though, for all those rewards!

Native to Mexico, dahlias were introduced to Europe in the late eighteenth century, though they were described two hundred years earlier by Francisco Hernandez, King Philip II of Spain's physician, who noted that natives used the hollow stems as water pipes, ate the tubers and even used the plants to treat epilepsy. In 1963, the dahlia became the national flower of Mexico.

GROWING

You can either buy potted dahlias ready to plant out once the frosts are over, or grow them from tubers. Buy tubers from reputable suppliers in winter and keep them in a dry place under cover until they begin to produce shoots. Once the shoots appear, pot them up and keep them inside until the plants are growing strongly and there's no longer any chance of frost. Choose a sunny spot in good, fertile, well-drained soil. Dig a generous hole, throw in plenty of well-rotted manure, bonemeal or container compost, then plant the tubers 10cm (4in) below the surface. Fill up the hole, tread down the compost, then water well. Border dahlias are low growing and self-supporting, but taller varieties will need staking. Do this now, when you plant the tuber.

Once the plants are established, encourage bushy growth by pinching out the main growing tips. Keep the plants well watered in dry spells and once they begin to flower, feed them every two to three weeks with a high-potash liquid feed. Deadhead any faded blooms to encourage the plant to produce more.

At the end of the season, cut the plants down to around 20cm (8in), then dig up the tubers, taking care not to damage them. Let them dry off naturally in a dry shed or greenhouse, then clean away any residual soil and trim any fine roots. Store the tubers in shallow wooden boxes or trays of dry sand or peat-free compost, leaving the crowns exposed. Keep them in a cool, dry, frost-free environment over winter. If they're in a shed,

you may need to cover them with newspaper during cold frosty periods. Check the tubers regularly and throw out any that are rotting or appear to be unhealthy.

PROBLEMS

Common pests include **aphids**, **capsid bugs**, **earwigs**, **caterpillars**, **red spider mite** and **slugs**. The plants can also fall victim to mildew, but this can be treated with spray fungicide.

CUTTING & CONDITIONING

Cut stems for arranging when the flowers are fully open, because buds will simply wither before opening when harvested. Make a horizontal cut using sharp secateurs, then plunge the stems into 5–7cm (2–3in) of very hot, almost boiling, water and leave them there for about an hour. This will help them to keep fresh in a vase for up to six days. Before arranging, strip off any leaves that will be below water level. Every two to three days, wash and cut another 2.5cm (1in) off each stem, before replacing them in fresh water. They look wonderful in all sorts of arrangements – see Summer table arrangement, page 195; Topiary tree, page 200; Pedestal, page 203.

DICENTRA

Dicentra spectabilis Hardy perennial

DIFFICULTY RATING: EASY

Delightful rows of the dangly heart-shaped flowers of this cottage-garden favourite have earned it many affectionate names, such as Bleeding Heart, Dutchman's Breeches, Lady's Locket and even Lady in the Bath! Plant three to five in your border and over the years they'll bring delightful colour to the garden from April right through to June. Being lovers of partial shade, some varieties make pretty woodland plants, or light up a gloomy corner of the garden. Their arching form and pretty, delicate, hand-like, lime-green leaves make them an excellent choice for cut flowers.

GROWING

Buy dicentra as plants then choose a lightly shaded site with deep, moist, but well-drained soil. Plant them 50cm (1½ft) apart. Keep the soil moist over the summer, then in the following April, apply a mulch to retain moisture and improve the soil. If after a few years they become overcrowded, you can lift and divide the clumps in autumn or spring, then re-plant them in new positions.

CUTTING & CONDITIONING

Cut the stems using sharp secateurs before arranging.

FOXGLOVE

Digitalis Hardy biennials and perennials
DIFFICULTY RATING: EASY

The stately purple spires of foxgloves look far too elegant for what is, after all, a wild flower that is often seen growing in softly shaded woodland or hedgerows. They've long been a mainstay of cottage gardens, hybridised by horticulturalists into endless variations of pink, purple, yellow, apricot, cream, plus pure white. Being biennials, foxgloves spend the first year growing leaves, with the flowers arriving in the second year, between June and August.

Foxgloves are happy self-seeders, although if you buy a cultivated or hybridised variety the new plants are likely to revert back to wild purple. For this reason, if you want plenty of cutting flowers for the least effort, your best plan could be to choose the original *Digitalis purpurea*. That way you could plant or sow seeds for two years in a row, then leave them to multiply naturally over the years, giving you plenty to cut whilst leaving some for the garden. If you are beguiled by the choice of stunning alternatives, that's still an option, though these will require a little more effort in that you'll need to germinate new seed each year.

GROWING

Ready-to-flower foxgloves can be bought from the garden centre, though this is an expensive option if you want to cut them for flower arranging as each plant produces a limited amount of spikes. Another option is to buy them as plugs, which might give you a dozen plants that should flower the following year. By far the cheapest option, though, is to buy seed.

Foxglove seeds are very small, so you'll get literally thousands in a packet.

You can either start them off under cover early in the year, then harden them off before planting out (see page 44), or, if you wait until all chance of frost is over, you can sow them straight into the ground. As the seeds are so tiny, you might want to mix them with fine sand to dilute them. Prepare a seedbed in a lightly shaded site and sow the seeds as finely as you can in drills 30cm (12in) apart. If space is limited, you can sow the seed where you want the plants to grow, but the results may not be as reliable. When the seedlings are large enough to handle, thin

them out to 15cm (6in) apart. In the autumn, they will be ready to go into their final planting positions 60cm (24in) apart, ready for flowering next year.

CUTTING & CONDITIONING

Always cut the central spike first as this will encourage the plant to send out more side flower spikes. Strip off any leaves and put the flowers in a bucket of warm water for an hour or two before arranging. Remove any of the lower flowers as they wilt. After a couple of days, cut the stems down and rearrange in fresh water.

GLADIOLI

Gladiolus Half-hardy perennials
DIFFICULTY RATING: EASY

Wonderfully showy and available in every colour and shade imaginable, it's no wonder gladioli are a natural favourite for the village show. Growing up to nearly 2m (6ft) tall, depending on the variety, their statuesque, almost theatrical flower spikes look striking in the garden. They also make an excellent cutting flower because they're both long lasting and provide structure to any arrangement (see Summer table arrangement, page 195). The range of flower sizes and endless colours are a major part of gladioli's fascination, and to make selection more manageable, an international system of classification has been developed using coded digits. Each variety has a three-figure number following it: the first indicates the size of the floret with 1 being miniature and 5 being giant. The next number indicates the colour; 1 for yellow, 8 for violet and 9 for smokies. The final number indicates how dark that colour is.

GROWING

The time to plant gladioli is when deciduous trees are well into leaf. Start by digging in well-rotted manure and, if your soil is very heavy, incorporate some sharp sand or gravel to improve the drainage. Choose corms that have a swelling around the root nodules, which is the sign that they are ready to plant and will thrive. Plant them 15cm (6in) deep with a minimum of 10cm (4in) between each corm. You should see signs of the first shoots growing through the soil about two or three weeks after planting.

Taller varieties will need staking. Drive a bamboo cane into the ground near the gladiolus, but clear of the corm so as not to damage it, then loosely tie in the spike using soft garden twine. Keep the area weed-free. Gladioli need around 2.5cm (1in) of water every week, so make sure you keep the soil fairly moist during dry periods with supplementary watering. Feed the plants every few weeks during their flowering period.

Gladioli corms will not survive northern European winters, and so they must be lifted no longer than six weeks after flowering, or once the leaves have started to brown. Remove them carefully with a garden fork so as to avoid damaging the corms, clean off the soil and cut the leaves down to 2.5cm (1in), then put the corms into a tray with a mesh bottom to dry them out. Put the trays into a well-ventilated space at a temperature of around 20°C (70°F).

Once the corms have dried, you can twist off the old ones to leave a clean basal scar. Also, remove any small offsets around the new corm to store separately as new plants to build up your stocks. All the corms should be stored root-side down in a single layer in shallow trays. Examine them periodically over the winter and discard any that show signs of rot or fungal disease.

CUTTING & CONDITIONING

When cutting gladioli, do not denude the plant as this will deplete the corm – they draw nutrition from the sun through their leaves, so always make sure there are at least four good-sized leaves left. Cut the flowers using sharp secateurs and strip off the bottom leaves before arranging.

HYDRANGEA 'ANNABELLE'

Hydrangea arborescens 'Annabelle' Shrub
DIFFICULTY RATING: EASY

The irresistible 'Annabelle' might not be a classic cutting flower, but any enthusiastic flower arranger who has grown one will put this hydrangea on their A1 must-have list. It produces an abundance of huge blooms that are 25cm (10in) across, which start off green and turn to frothy white throughout the summer. There are so many and they often weigh down the plant so much that there's no dilemma as to whether or not you cut – just go ahead! They look wonderful three or five to a vase (or even just one to a bottle-type vase), or as a focal flower in a big showy arrangement. See page 204 for the Christmas wreath, page 199 for the Hanging floral design and page 203 for the Pedestal arrangement.

Hydrangea 'Annabelle' is such a pretty shrub with magnificent blooms that it's hard to believe it is native to the east coast of North America and not some painstakingly developed cultivar. Being a native, it is naturally hardy and can survive both hard winters and cutting down to the ground, returning the next year to produce another flush of showy blooms.

GROWING

Buy young plants in containers and plant them in a sheltered, partially shaded site in moist, fertile, but well-drained soil. Although the experts say 'Annabelle' can also be planted in a sunny site, she can very quickly wilt within a few hours on hot days and will need regular watering. Water at the roots in the evening or early morning, avoiding the leaves or they will scorch on sunny days. Unlike most hydrangeas, the arborescens group blooms on new wood, which is why these plants can be cut down in the autumn. However, cutting 'Annabelle' right down to the base results in very bendy stems and the blooms can become weighed down to ground level, especially if there's been heavy rain. The stems will strengthen and thicken if you prune to about 45–60cm (18–24in) in autumn, which will give more (but slightly smaller) blooms. If you live in a very cold area, these might not survive the winter, so you'd be best to cut them down a bit harder.

CUTTING & CONDITIONING

Use sharp secateurs, cut the stems at a 45-degree angle so rainwater runs off them. Give them a good drink in a bucket of water for a couple of hours before arranging. Cut to length again, at a 45-degree angle, to encourage good uptake of water.

IRIS

Iris Hardy perennial

DIFFICULTY RATING: MEDIUM

Available in a fabulous array of colours, sword-leaved irises lend an elegant architectural element to the garden, and also give great structure and form to any flower arrangement. There are many different iris divisions; some that grow in bogs or near water and others that are alpine, but the easiest to grow and the best for cutting are the bearded and crested types.

GROWING

Choose a well-drained sunny site and dig in some general fertiliser, then prepare a hole large enough to accommodate the rhizome (the fleshy 'roots' at the base of the plant) so that the top surface is partly exposed, planting the irises about 30cm (12in) apart. Firm the soil around the rhizome and water in. Do not mulch as this will keep the soil too moist and rot the rhizome.

The rhizomes will propagate by growing 'daughter' rhizomes and eventually the original rhizome will rot. If the irises become overcrowded after about three years or so, divide the rhizomes and re-plant them either to enlarge the clump, or to move to another part of the garden. The time to do this is about six weeks after they finish flowering. Lift the rhizome and, using a sharp knife, cut away a fan of leaves along with a portion of rhizome. Throw away any old, withered or rotted rhizomes and keep the largest and healthiest-looking ones. Cut the leaves down to about 15cm (6in), and trim the roots, then replant the rhizomes as above.

CUTTING & CONDITIONING

Irises are not hugely long lasting in a vase, so cut them when they are still in bud. Use a sharp pair of secateurs and cut them as low down as possible. Don't denude any one plant: they draw nutrition from the sun through their leaves, so leave at least four healthy leaves on each plant.

JAPANESE ANEMONE

Anemone hupehensis Hardy perennial

DIFFICULTY RATING: EASY

Bobbing high on stems of up to 1m (3ft), these delightful simple white or pink daisy-like flowers cheer the garden from August right through to October. Once they're established, there will be plenty for cutting, and with their long, elegant stems they're great candidates for flower arranging.

GROWING

Buy Japanese anemones as strong plants from the garden centre and plant them in a semi-shaded site in rich soil. If you have a small garden, buy only one plant, because it will spread. Anemones need to be watered well in the first year. Although this is a hardy perennial, it might not survive very cold winters. In colder areas, do not cut your Japanese anemones down in autumn; the stems will provide protection over the winter.

CUTTING & CONDITIONING

Give the stems a good soak in a bucket of water before arranging.

LAVENDER

Lavandula Shrub

DIFFICULTY RATING: MEDIUM

This distinctive aromatic plant barely needs introduction. Its elegant indigo spikes of flowers grow above silvery grey or green foliage, bringing life to the garden all year round. There are several different groups of lavender, but the most obvious division is between the classic *L. angustifolia*, and the earlier-flowering *L. stoechas*, or French lavender, which has a few characteristic tufty bracts on every bloom. With abundant flowers from June right through to August, if you grow *L. angustifolia* there's plenty to cut for beautiful flower arrangements that will perfume the room. Bees love lavender, so this is a great plant to grow in the vegetable garden to encourage efficient pollination of your crops.

GROWING

Native to the Mediterranean, lavender loves a sunny site and thrives even in fairly poor, well-drained soil, Don't be tempted to dig in extra compost, because if you do the plants are more likely to grow spindly and weak.

Buy young lavender plants or plugs and water them well just before planting, allowing time for the water to drain through. Dig a generous hole and line it with sharp sand for extra drainage, then remove the plant from the pot and place it in the centre, making sure the top of the compost aligns with ground level. Fill around the plant with soil, press down firmly with your fingers, then water well. The plants should be positioned about 45–90cm (18–36in) apart or, if you want a hedge, slightly closer at 30–40cm (12–16in).

Water young plants about three times a week for the first summer, but after that these drought-resistant plants should be fine just being left to get on with it. At the end of the summer, prune the plants hard by cutting down into 2.5cm (1in) of the current year's growth. If the plants have got a bit leggy, prune them a bit harder, but make sure there is plenty of foliage left as new leaves don't readily sprout from old wood.

Well-tended and pruned lavender bushes will live for around 15 years. If you inherit neglected bushes that have become leggy and woody, you could try pruning them very hard down to just above some new shots in the old wood. They may well respond and reward you with new invigorated growth, but if not, you're likely to be fighting a losing battle, so remove them and start again with new plants. Stoechas lavender should be pruned at the end of August by cutting off one-third of the stems.

CUTTING & CONDITIONING

Simply cut off the flower stems using sharp secateurs and arrange immediately.

LILY

Lilium Bulb

DIFFICULTY RATING: DIFFICULT

The classic florist's flower, lilies have it all: they're tall, stately and elegant, come in exquisite white or a range of pinks, oranges and yellows and smell like heaven! They have a reputation for being difficult to grow because they are prone to fungal diseases, though some of the newer varieties are less vulnerable. Lilies can also be tricky because some like acid (ericaceous) soil and some don't. Happy in pots, this can be the best way to grow them because they can be moved around to the sunny sites they love and be planted in the right soil.

GROWING

Lily bulbs can be planted any time from autumn right through to spring, though October is ideal. Most lilies produce their roots just above the bulb, and will need 15cm (6in) soil above them. The planting distance between them depends on the size of the variety, so consult the packaging.

Although lilies can be grown in the ground outside, they are more manageable in containers. For example, if you want to force Asiatic varieties, such as the florist's favourite, *L. longiflorum*, it should be brought under cover six weeks after planting. Lilies can be fussy in winter; in mild climates many are hardy and need a cool outdoor winter to produce a good show of flowers in the summer. Others, however, need protection through cold winters, so wrap pots in bubble wrap or horticultural fleece to protect the roots from frost. Ideally, overwinter all lilies in a light, cool, but frost-free place, such as a cold frame

or greenhouse. When planting, check whether the variety needs ericaceous compost (see page 40), if not, multipurpose compost or John Innes No3 is ideal. You'll need deep containers of at least 25cm (10in) diameter, which offer enough space for one large bulb or two to three smaller bulbs. Put a layer of broken crocks in the bottom of the pot, then for those lilies that form roots above the bulb, cover with compost to a height of two and a half times the height of the bulb. For some species, such as the Asiatics, whose roots form below the bulb, cover with compost to a height exactly matching that of the bulb. Top with soil that has slow-release fertiliser granules mixed in. Keep the pots moist at all times, but don't overwater, and feed them every fortnight with liquid tomato fertiliser. After flowering, once the foliage has died down, re-pot the bulbs with fresh compost for a good crop of flowers next year.

PROBLEMS

Red lily beetles and their larvae chomp through lily leaves, leaving a denuded plant that looks unsightly and has undersized bulbs. In spring and early summer, check under the leaves for egg masses, which can be red-orange or brown. Also look out for larvae – these are hard to spot because they'll be charmingly hiding under their own poo! If there are only a few affected leaves, just pick them off whole and destroy them. If there are too many, clean the leaves, wearing disposable gloves, or if the plant is infested, spray it with

a biological spray incorporating neem oil (see page 79). Any larvae that survive will drop down into the soil to pupate and emerge later as the distinctive red lily beetles. Hunt and destroy any adults immediately. They're pretty speedy on their pins and drop off onto their backs into the soil where they're difficult to spot because their legs and undercarriages are black. Outwit them by holding a jar of soapy water under the 'host' leaf and nudge the beetle in! It is important to empty the pots the lillies were grown in at the end of the year and scrub them out.

CUTTING & CONDITIONING

Cut the flower stems as low as you wish, but don't denude the plant as this will sap its energy. Strip off any leaves that will sit below the water line of the vase, and give the flowers a good drink in a bucket of water for at least an hour before arranging.

LOVE-IN-A-MIST

Nigella damascena Hardy annual
DIFFICULTY RATING: EASY

Pretty blue flowers surrounded by a veil of feathery foliage – little wonder this traditional cottage flower was given its romantic country name. For very little effort it will produce endless blooms all summer long if a regime of deadheading and re-sowing every week is carried out. If that wasn't enough, at the end of the summer *Nigella* obligingly transforms any leftover flowers into delightful lantern-like seedheads, and if you leave some on the plant, they'll readily self-seed and reward you with another swathe of delicate blue the following year.

GROWING

Ever-so-easy seeds simply need to be sprinkled in position in spring, once the frosts are over (or, if you're organised enough, in the autumn) and they'll do the rest. You can collect the seed if you want at the end of the year (see page 88), or just leave the plants to self-seed.

CUTTING & CONDITIONING

Use scissors to cut blooms whenever you want. Strip off the lower leaves before arranging. The seedheads make delightful additions to arrangements, too, so you can keep on cutting right the way through to autumn.

MARIGOLD

Calendula officinalis Short-lived perennial, usually grown as a hardy annual

DIFFICULTY RATING: EASY

This delightful, daisy-like pot marigold in cheery oranges and yellows has been grown as a cottage-garden herb for centuries, traditionally valued for its pharmaceutical properties, which earned it the common name 'Mary's Gold'. Easy to cultivate, it is a great choice for children who want to grow their own flowers.

GROWING

The easy-to-handle, crescent-shaped seeds can be sown straight into the ground once the frosts are over, or start them off earlier under cover (see page 46). Calendula will cheerfully grow almost anywhere. Sow them about 7–10cm (3–4in) apart, about 0.5cm (¼in) deep. Water when necessary over the summer.

CUTTING & CONDITIONING

Strip off the lower leaves and give the flowers a drink before arranging.

MARIGOLD

Tagetes Half-hardy annual, perennial

DIFFICULTY RATING: EASY

These are often called 'French' or 'African' marigolds, which is misleading because tagetes originate from neither country. They are native to Mexico, where they have huge cultural significance for mourning, and are used abundantly as a decoration for Day of the Dead festivals.

For the gardener, marigolds' most useful role is as companion plant extraordinaire in the vegetable patch. Their pungent smell naturally deters pests that range from flying insects to root-eating nematodes, and even small rodents, and in doing so they bring lightness, brightness and cheeriness when planted between the crops. However, they also exude antibacterial properties from their roots and so should not be planted near legumes such as beans and peas as they will interfere with their nitrogen-fixing abilities. Growing to between 30cm (12in) and 1m (3ft) high, tagetes range from the dainty single flowers of *T. patula*, the 'official' French marigold, to the blousy double 12.5cm (5in) blooms of *T. erecta* 'Doubloon', one of the so-called African marigolds.

GROWING

Tagetes prefers a sunny site and will obligingly thrive in almost any soil. Start the seeds off under cover in spring, or plant out potted young plants directly into the ground once the frosts are over. Once the seedlings appear, thin to about 30cm (12in) apart. Pinch out the growing tips to encourage a bushy habit and water and deadhead regularly to encourage more blooms.

CUTTING & CONDITIONING

Cutting spurs the plant on to produce more flowers, so don't be shy with the secateurs. Strip off the lower leaves of cut stems and give the flowers a drink of cool water for an hour before arranging.

MICHAELMAS DAISY

Aster novae-angliae and *A. novi-belgii* Perennial
DIFFICULTY RATING: EASY

This pretty range of purple, pink, mauve or indigo daisies is a thoroughly welcome sight, coming, as it does, at the end of September like a floral full stop to summer, then enthusiastically continuing to bloom through autumn – sometimes even well into November. They have a charming informality, with flowers that range from the most delicate singles to doubles that could be mistaken for chrysanthemums. The plant we normally associate with Michaelmas is tall, carrying flowers almost 1m (3ft) off the ground, and these are the best for cutting (see Summer table arrangement, page 195).

GROWING

Michaelmas daisies are not fussy customers; they'll bloom and grow in almost any soil, and can be seen, self-seeded, wherever they can get a roothold, such as in deserted railway cuttings or clinging to the edges of footpaths. You might get more blooms if you dig in some compost, though if you overdo it the heads could get too heavy for the stems and you'll end up needing to stake them. Michaelmas daisies can be prone to mildew, but good garden hygiene will help protect against this.

CUTTING & CONDITIONING

Cut Michaelmas daisies can last up to a fortnight in a vase. Prepare them by stripping off any leaves that will be below the water line, and take off every other leaf a little higher up.

NASTURTIUM

Tropaeolum majus Hardy annuals and perennials

DIFFICULTY RATING: EASY

Merry orange, red and yellow nasturtiums come in many forms, from climbers and trailers to bedding dwarfs, most with their distinctive limey-green, lily-pad-style leaves. They're a joy to grow in containers, window boxes, climbing through hedges, or plain and simple in the border, bringing colour to the garden well into autumn. Nasturtiums are easy to grow, and are very useful companion plants for the vegetable patch. They also have delicious seeds.

GROWING

Nasturtiums can be sown outside once the frosts are over. Their large seeds are easy to handle so this is one the children can help with. Nasturtiums like a sunny site in well-drained, not-too-rich soil. Rake the soil and sow the seeds about 25cm (10in) apart and 0.5cm (¼in) deep. Water regularly and they'll do the rest themselves. Deadhead them regularly to keep the flowers coming.

CUTTING & CONDITIONING

Use scissors to cut the flowers for arranging, being careful not to cut into any other part of the plant. Give them a drink for an hour before arranging.

COMPANION PLANTING

Ironically, one of the main reasons you should plant nasturtiums in the garden is because black aphids, blackfly and cabbage white butterflies can't resist them. They are their number one choice for dinner! Not such a good look,

maybe, but the pests will zoom in on the nasturtiums and (you hope), leave your crops alone. That way, you have all the pests in one place, which makes them easier to eradicate.

There are several ways to do this, and you need to plan your campaign. Early in the year, when the pests first arrive, cut off the affected leaves and dispose of them. This will eradicate the first generation of pests, breaking the breeding cycle. The next solution is to bring on reinforcements in the form of ladybirds and their larvae to eat the aphids. They may arrive on their own, or you could order them on the internet through a biological control site. The ladybirds (or their larvae) will arrive through the post complete with their own popcorn lunchbox (see page 77). Set them to work immediately.

Alternatively, you could spray the plants with a biological pesticide that includes neem oil

(see page 79). Finally, if none of that suits, once the plants are really infested you can cut them down and permanently dispose of them by burning them or rotting them in black plastic bags. The plants will probably re-grow (depending on the time of year and weather conditions) and may even be pest-free for the rest of the season because the breeding cycle will have been interrupted.

ROSES

Rosa Shrub

DIFFICULTY RATING: EASY

Exquisitely beautiful and sweetly perfumed, the rose has been an icon of romance since the ancient civilisations of Babylonia and Assyria. Then, the choice was limited to a few wild species and their natural hybrids, some of which were brought back to Europe with the Crusades. Even with a limited choice, roses were linked with romance, including *Rosa mundi*, which is still available today. The legend goes that it is named after fair Rosamund, the murdered mistress of England's twelfth-century king, Henry II, who ordered that every year, on the anniversary of her death, her grave should be swathed in this exquisite pink-striped double rose. Roses clearly continued to be significant through the centuries, with the Tudor Rose, dating back to 1485, becoming England's national symbol. However, it wasn't until the early nineteenth-century, when cultivated roses were brought back from China,

that breeders began crossing them to create a dizzying array of types and varieties.

There is now a profusion of varieties and only rose professionals, or lifetime hobbyists, have a really clear understanding of the subtle differences between them.

The aim here is to give a basic understanding of the different types, and highlight the all-time award-winning favourites.

FLOWER TYPES

There are many reasons why you might want to choose a particular

rose. Some flower all summer, some just produce one fantastic flush; some are shrubs, others like to climb; some are perfumed, some are not; some have interesting rosehips, others don't produce any. That apart, there are basically eight different types of flower shapes to choose from – which come in endless colours.

Of course, what we'd all like is a rose in an awesome colour with a heady perfume that flowers abundantly all summer, produces interesting rosehips, is disease-free and doesn't have thorns. But it doesn't work like that. Put simplistically, the original (species) roses produce a single abundant flush of exquisitely perfumed blooms, followed by interesting hips, but they tend to be disease prone and thorny. In developing hybrids, many breeders aim to produce roses that are resistant to disease and either bloom several times in the season or flower perpetually through the summer right until the first frosts. However, the cost of this is that the resulting rose is sterile, which means it can't produce rosehips and doesn't have so strong a perfume. The wide choice became so complex that in Victorian times roses were categorised into types. Since then, with new varieties being bred each year, those categories became blurred and have now been reduced to three main types: Wild Roses, Old Garden Roses and Modern Garden Roses, and within those groups you'll come across several sub groups. For simplicity, all you really need to know is explained in the A–Z.

AN A–Z OF ROSES

Climbers produce trusses of blooms on stems that are stiffer than ramblers (see below). Some produce only a single flush of flowers over the summer, others flower right up to the first frosts. Modern hybrids need training against a wall, but only light pruning (see Pruning, page 178).

Floribundas are a cross between Polyanthus and Hybrid Teas and have large trusses of many flowers on each stem. They keep blooming all summer long and are hardier than the Hybrid Teas.

Hybrid Teas are a cross between Tea Roses and Hybrid Perpetuals. These shrubs can be rigid and upright, and produce large elegant flowers during the course of the summer. They're often disease resistant but don't have a strong perfume, but even so they are favourites amongst show roses.

Miniature Roses are modern hybrids with small blooms and leaves which never grow higher than 38cm (15in). They're used for edging beds, in rockeries and containers.

Modern Garden Roses include any roses that do not come into the categories of Wild nor Old. They include the

Hybrid Teas, Floribundas, most Climbers, Patios, Miniatures and Polyanthus. Traditionally, these had less scent than Old Roses, but new hybrids with more fragrance are now being introduced. Modern Roses are generally more disease resistant than Old Roses.

Old Garden Roses generally bloom only once a year, usually in June and through to July, after which they form attractive rosehips. The flowers generally have an exquisite perfume. They are mainly shrub roses and these are divided into different kinds, such as Alba, Bourbon, Damask, Gallica and Tea. There are a few climbing roses in this category too.

Patio Roses are small, neat shrubs bearing sprays of flowers all summer.

Polyanthus are tough, repeat-flowering shrubs with many small flowers. The trailing and spreading varieties are often used for groundcover.

Wild Roses are the original species roses, and hybrids of these share most of the parent characteristics. They flower only once and generally have simple blooms with just a few petals. They can be very thorny and less disease resistant than other types. Wild Roses are often used for rootstock, which means they provide the roots onto which the rose of choice is grafted. Sometimes the rootstock sends out a shoot, which is called a sucker. You can recognise this because they are thorny and will almost certainly have different leaves to the rest of the plant.

Ramblers have been around since Victorian times. They are similar to climbers but have clusters of single blooms on flexible stems and are often viciously thorny. They flower on new wood, so you need to cut away old stems every autumn.

Shrub Roses have self-supporting stems, as opposed to Climbers and Ramblers, which need support.

Species and **Species hybrids** are the original wild roses and their immediate hybrids. They usually flower just once, in June, and have a great perfume and interesting rosehips.

Tea Roses originally came from China. Their blooms have an elegant pointed shape and an exquisite perfume.

FLOWER SHAPES

Roses come in many shapes and sizes; from tiny single blooms with only four petals to large, elegant, pointed Hybrid Teas and cabbage-like fully double rosettes that have over 30 petals. Below are the main shapes, which can be single, semi-double, double or fully double, depending on the amount of petals they have.

Cupped – open flowers with the petals curving inwards. These can be single or double, but all display the anthers in the middle.

Flat – open single or semi-double

blooms and you can see the pollen-producing anthers in the middle.
Pointed – typical Hybrid Tea shape with a high, tight centre. Can be semi-double to fully-double.
Pompon – small rounded blooms with small, tightly packed petals. Double or fully double.
Rosette – flat double or fully-double shape. Can also be quartered where the inner petals make four distinct sections.
Urn – typically Hybrid Tea shape, but not so pointed. Semi-double to fully double.

BUYING

You can buy and plant container-grown roses at any time of the year, as long as the ground you are planting into is not saturated or frosted. Between October and March you can also buy bare-root plants, which is more cost effective. These will need to be planted as soon as you receive them, or at least heeled into a trench or a pot until the final position is ready for planting.

PLANTING

Soak bare-roots in a bucket of water for at least an hour before planting. Use sharp secateurs to cut off any dead wood, any leaves on the stems and trim any roots that are damaged or over 30cm (12in) long. Dig a large hole that is 45cm (10in) deep and will accommodate the roots when they are spread out. Place the plant in the hole so that the join of the rose to the rootstock is 2.5cm (1in) below ground level. Now fill around the roots with the excavated soil with a little bonemeal added, firm in and water well. Mulch to conserve moisture and keep the weeds down. Water regularly, especially in the first year, then once the plant is fully established, water during dry periods and apply a rose-type fertiliser twice during the growing season.

PRUNING

In late winter or early spring, prune shrub roses, standards and climbers just when the new growth is beginning to show. Start by cutting out dead wood and any branches that cross so that you can encourage an open, outward habit, which will ensure good air circulation around the plant. To prune, use sharp secateurs and make a sloping cut immediately above a bud and angled away from it so that the rainfall falls away. Hybrid Teas and Floribundas should be cut back to about 15cm (6in) high to encourage a strong bushy growth. In future years, just cut the branches back to about half their length. Do not prune strong healthy stems of old shrub roses unless they get leggy and you want to improve the shape of the plant.

In autumn, prune back ramblers once they have finished flowering. For other roses, cut back any dead wood and long shoots that might be blown around over winter and could damage the plants.

TRAINING CLIMBERS

Prepare the wall or fence by fixing strong garden galvanised wire at 50cm (18in) vertical intervals. Fan-training encourages the rose to grow over a large area on the wall to create a pleasing shape with flowers at all levels. Do this by training the main shoots horizontally, because that way they send up the flower-bearing shoots. Tie in the main shoots using soft garden string. In the early years of training, while you are still encouraging more main shoots to grow horizontally, when you are spring pruning you may want to untie the whole plant, re-tying it into a more pleasing shape.

PROBLEMS

Roses are susceptible to many pests and diseases, and the best plan is to buy a disease-resistant variety. Even so, they are likely to be infested by aphids and prone to **black spot**, a fungal disease. Strong plants have the best chance of resisting and recovering from these, so keep the ground weed free and water and feed them appropriately.

Aphids should be squashed between your fingers as soon as you spot any. Failing that, use biological controls such as biological pesticide incorporating neem oil, or ladybirds, which, if

they don't naturally arrive to nosh those aphids, can be ordered over the internet (see page 77).

Cut off any leaves that show **black spot** and either burn them or seal them in a plastic bag before disposing of them. In the autumn, clear away any fallen leaves that may harbour the pupae of pests or fungal pores.

CUTTING & CONDITIONING

Cut roses for arranging in the same way as you would prune them, making clean diagonal cuts away from a bud. Immediately plunge them into a bucket of water for an hour. When you're ready to arrange them, cut the stems at a 45-degree angle to allow for maximum water uptake. They look wonderful in simple or more complicated arrangements – see Summer wreath, page 196; Hanging floral design, page 199 and Summer table arrangement, page 195.

SIX FAILSAFE FAVOURITES

Well, let's be honest, when it comes to gardening, nothing can be absolutely failsafe, but here's a list of award-winning, tried-and-true, old favourite roses.

Felicia is a hybrid musk Floribunda rose that produces abundant flushes of apricot-tinged pink blooms in June and then again in September. It is disease resistant.

Graham Thomas is an old-style, faintly-scented, Modern, yellow, rosette-cupped double rose. With good disease resistance, it produces a flush of blooms in summer and then again in autumn.

Iceberg is a very popular Floribunda bush rose that is also available as a climber, producing sprays of fully double, cupped flowers set against vibrant green leaves all through the summer right up until the first frosts. It has only a few thorns.

New Dawn is a pretty, perfumed, palest-pink climber that produces generous flushes of blooms in clusters along its branches in summer and then again in autumn. It will even thrive on a north-facing wall.

Rosa Mundi, with its distinctive, stripy, pink, semi-double, flat blooms dates back to before 1581 and is remarkably disease resistant for an Old Garden Rose. Its delicately perfumed blooms adorn the garden in a single flush in June.

Royal William is a red Hybrid Tea with a subtle perfume that produces beautiful blooms all through the summer.

SCABIOUS

Scabiosa Perennial

DIFFICULTY RATING: EASY

Producing pretty blue pincushion blooms on long slim stems from June until the first frosts, scabious is a must-have for the flower arranger. Their buds are also delightful, looking like mini pincushions, which add further interest both to the border and to arrangements. Plant a group of three or five of these cottage-garden favourites and they'll reward you with blooms all summer long, year after year.

GROWING

Buy these in containers from the garden centre and plant them in a well-drained sunny site. Keep them weed-free and watered during dry periods – and let them get on with it!

CUTTING & CONDITIONING

Cutting the flowers encourages them to produce more, so don't hold back! They should be cut using sharp secateurs or scissors and put straight into a bucket of water. Cut them to length before arranging.

STATICE

Limonium sinuatum Half-hardy perennial grown as an annual

DIFFICULTY RATING: EASY

Also known as sea lavender, this is particularly popular with flower arrangers as it flowers abundantly from July to September and can be used both fresh and dried. They're easy to dry and, unlike many flowers, in the process retain much of their original shades of pink, purple, yellow and white.

GROWING

Raise seed under cover, then plant out after all danger of frost has passed in a sunny spot at 30cm (12in) spacings in well-drained, light or medium soil. Keep weed-free and watered throughout the growing season.

CUTTING & CONDITIONING

Cut the flowers early in the morning before the heat of the midday sun and before they are fully open. If you are going to use them for fresh arrangements, strip off the lower leaves, then plunge them straight into a bucket of water. Cut the stems to length before arranging. If you want to dry them, strip off the lower leaves, then make up bunches of up to six stems, securing them with rubber bands, and hang them upside down in a cool, well-ventilated place.

SUNFLOWERS

Helianthus annuus Hardy annual

DIFFICULTY RATING: EASY

SWEET PEAS

Lathyrus odoratus Hardy annual

DIFFICULTY RATING: MEDIUM

Sunflowers in their wonderful shades range from brightest yellow through all the copper hints to almost chocolatey brown! As well as the giants, there are loads of smaller varieties to choose from, but it's the big ones we love and that astound us every year in August as we crane our necks up to look at the 3m (10ft) giants, grown from seeds planted just a few months previously.

GROWING

Choose a sunny position (preferably in April or May), then push the seeds 2.5cm (1in) straight into the ground where they will grow. Plant them at 60cm (2ft) intervals, water, then watch them grow! Tall ones may need staking.

CUTTING & CONDITIONING

Cut the stem down to the ground, cut to length, strip off the lower leaves and plunge into a bucket of water until you're ready to arrange them. They add impact and height to an arrangement, see Pedestal, page 203; Topiary tree, page 200.

The watercolour shades and heady perfume of sweet peas make them a cottage-garden favourite from June to October. With their long straight stems, they're a flower arranger's must-have.

GROWING

Soak sweet pea seeds in tepid water before sowing to get them off to a good start, then sow indoors about 1cm (½in) deep in seed trays and water well. Once the shoots appear, put them in a bright sunny position and pinch out the tops to encourage a bushy habit. When the risk of frost has passed, harden them off ready for planting out. Choose a sunny position and dig in plenty of well-rotted manure. You'll need to arrange a support structure of between 30cm and 2.5m (1–8ft), depending on the variety. Plant the sweet peas in groups of three 15cm (6in) apart. Keep the bed weed-free and well watered.

CUTTING & CONDITIONING

The more you cut sweet peas, the more flowers they produce, so cut what you can for flower arranging and deadhead any that you miss. Use florist's scissors to cut the stems, plunging them straight into a bucket of water. Cut the stems to length when arranging. See Hand-tied bouquet, page 192.

TOBACCO PLANT

Nicotiana Half-hardy annuals and perennials

DIFFICULTY RATING: EASY

Sweet-smelling *Nicotiana* is native to tropical and sub-tropical areas of North and South America, but it is hardy enough to enjoy northern European summers too! These slightly raggedy flowers in white, pinks or burgundy grow to about 1m (3ft) high and look wonderful planted in drifts in the border. At night they exude their beguiling perfume, so plant them near the barbecue area!

GROWING

As they come from a warm climate, sowing *Nicotiana* outside, even after the frosts have finished, is not an option. It's better to buy established plants from the garden centre and plant them out at 30cm (12in) spacings. If you would like to raise lots from seed you'll need to do that in the greenhouse (see page 46) and harden them off (see page 44) before planting them in the ground. Keep the plants watered during periods of drought.

CUTTING & CONDITIONING

Use secateurs to cut the flowers, then strip off the lower leaves and put them in a bucket of water for at least an hour before arranging.

ZINNIA

Zinnia elegans Half-hardy annual
DIFFICULTY RATING: MEDIUM

Zingy zinnias in their summer-bright pinks, oranges, yellows and even lime greens are gloriously extrovert, exploding colour into the garden from the end of summer right up until the first frosts. These daisy-like flowers are at their best when showing off their middles, though some people prefer the fully double varieties that have dahlia-like appeal. Natives of Mexico and the southern states of North America, zinnias do best in warm dry summers.

GROWING

Zinnias germinate at 23–26°C (74–80°F), so in Britain it is essential that you raise the seed under glass. If you don't have a greenhouse, you could do this in a heated propagator on the windowsill, or seal the planted-up seed tray in a plastic bag and put it on the windowsill. Sow them onto seed compost then cover with a layer of compost 3mm (⅛in) deep. They should germinate in a week to a fortnight. When the seedlings are big enough to handle, prick them out into 7.5cm (3in) pots (see page 43) and harden them off (see page 44) until they are ready to go into the ground well after the last frosts. Plant them out in a sunny site 30cm (12in) apart.

PROBLEMS

Zinnias can be prone to **mildew**, so make sure they get plenty of ventilation and don't be tempted to overcrowd them. Don't overwater them.

CUTTING & CONDITIONING

The more you cut, the more they flower, so cut zinnias as you need them, stripping off the leaves as you go and plunging them into a bucket of water. Cut zinnias to length to arrange. See Hand-tied bouquet, page 192.

The main dilemma most gardeners have when it comes to cutting flowers is that you can't have it both ways – you want them in the house, but you don't want to denude the garden of those precious blooms. The solution is to grow some as a crop. A few packets of carefully chosen seeds won't cost much but they could give you plenty to cut right through the summer and autumn until the first frosts. The A–Z guide that starts on page 156 offers a selection of the most productive flowers and how to grow them.

HARVESTING

The best time to cut flowers is in the morning, when most of the dew has evaporated, but before they have lost too much moisture in the heat of the midday sun. Most flowers are best harvested when the buds are just about to burst.

You will need a sharp pair of secateurs or florist's scissors and a large bucket of water. Cut the stems as long as possible, making clean cuts to avoid damaging the plant. Strip off the lower leaves to reduce moisture loss,

then immediately plunge the flower into the water. Keep each kind of flower in a group to make choosing them for arrangement easier.

CONDITIONING

To help prolong their life, bring the flowers into a cool place and give them a good long drink before arranging, ideally leaving them overnight. Fill a large bucket or basin with tepid water, giving every stem plenty of space. Cut the stems to 45 degrees, to help them take in more water, and strip off any leaves that may be below the water line. Bash the last 2.5cm (1in) or so of woody stems to help the uptake of water.

Always add commercial flower food to the water, as this greatly prolongs the life of all cut flowers by replacing minerals and nutrients, and also prevents bacteria from forming in the water. Remove any flowers that have gone over and cut down the stems to give the whole arrangement a new lease of life. Some flowers are quite greedy drinkers so check water levels regularly. (Some flowers fare best with specific conditioning methods, see individual entries in the A–Z.)

Florist's wire is available on reels, or in cut lengths, known as 'stub wires'. Both come in a range of gauges. The most useful range from heavy, which is 1.25mm thick (18 gauge) to finer 0.71mm thick (22 gauge). There are also much finer gauge wires, down to 32 gauge, which professional florists use for more intricate work. Wire can also be used to prepare materials such as fruits, vegetables, pine cones or eggshells. Take a length of wire and pass it through one end of the object, until both ends are the same length, then twist them together to make a wire 'stem' ready for use.

Florist's tape comes in two forms: anchor tape, which is used to hold florist's foam in position, and stem tape, which is a self-sealing crepe paper tape for making bouquets and finishing corsages, and also for covering ugly wires.

DRYING FLOWERS

By the end of the summer, some flowers naturally begin to dry out and, with a little help, can be fully dried so they retain their colours. These include lavender, cornflowers, bells of Ireland (mollucella), statice and yarrow, which can be used for everlasting arrangements. For dried flowers, always cut them late morning after the dew has evaporated but before the sun gets too hot. Make them up into bunches of five to ten stems and secure with elastic bands. Hang them up in a warm well-ventilated room or shed away from direct sunlight until fully dry.

The best time to cut flowers is in the morning, when most of the dew has evaporated, but before they have lost too much moisture in the heat of the midday sun.

FLORIST'S BASIC TOOLKIT

If you love the look of flowers put simply in vases of water, all you really need is a sharp pair of secateurs or florist's scissors. If you want to make more formal arrangements, you'll need a little more...

Florist's foam makes an easy job of positioning and holding flowers where you want them. It is available as bricks, rings, cones and spheres in various sizes. There are two types: brown for dry arrangements and green for fresh. The green foam must be soaked before use. Simply put it in a large basin of water, allowing it to soak unhindered, as it absorbs the water it will sink, indicating it is soaked through. Always add flower food to the water as you soak the foam, as this fills it with goodness and energy.

FLOWERS THROUGH THE SEASONS

SPRING

Spring starts slowly but lavishly, decking bare trees with pussy willow, dancing catkins and generous garlands of white and pink blossoms, all of which look wonderful casually arranged in large jugs or vases. The blossoms are soon followed by vibrant colour: the vivid sunshine yellows, azure blues, pinks and vibrant reds of spring bulbs.

SUMMER

The boundary between late spring and early summer is a blurred one. Sometimes the changeover is slow, over several weeks, but sometimes, in just one hot sunny weekend, the garden seems to burst into the full bloom of summer and a crescendo of colour brightens every corner. The variety of shapes and sizes is also astounding, offering plenty of material for endless arrangements. Grow cut flowers as crops, choosing your favourite from the A–Z section (pages 108–183) and you'll have plenty to bring into the house all summer, all (almost) for free.

AUTUMN

Of all the seasons, autumn is the most bountiful. By the end of the summer, when the main flush of flowers is over, the garden can look a little overgrown, and then along comes a whole new crew of flamboyant blooms like sunflowers, dahlias, chrysanthemums and asters, jostling for attention in the garden with their extrovert colours. They're joined by fruits, berries and architectural seedheads for what looks like an end of year party of colour and form.

WINTER

Rich red berries and full evergreen foliage are winter's classic colours. As winter progresses, you'll be able to add in white touches using mistletoe, Christmas roses (hellebores) and snowdrops. The key to success here is to work with a variety of foliage. Look for blue-tinged fir, variegated holly and ivy and, especially early in winter, the last of the red-tinged autumn leaves, or even naturally skeletonised leaves. Team these with whatever berries you can find, such as holly and any hips and haws.

Seeing all the wonderful flowers in the allotments in such profusion on the programme will make people realise that anyone can grow and enjoy flowers. You don't even have to have a garden – you can cultivate them in pots on the patio.

Picking flowers you've grown yourself is an easy way to reconnect with nature. People today live in fairly sterile environments, and all you need is a few flowers to energise a room. In my home, I keep them simple in old shabby chic jugs or containers – they're just beautiful left alone! But as a floral designer, I love to use flowers theatrically to deliver a real wow factor. Through teaching classes for over 20 years, I realised people want to know all the classic flower arranging techniques to create a wide range of contemporary and classic designs suitable for their own homes, special events and occasions.

If you are reluctant to denude the garden by picking flowers, have a cutting area, or grow them between vegetables. It can save you a lot of money, especially at the expensive times of the year when flowers are hard to come by. A packet of seeds costs about £1, but saves you many times that in bought bunches. Home-grown garden flowers have a unique personality, unlike mass-produced commercial crops. Flowers are a real recession buster, so have a go and be creative.

Meet the Expert

JONATHAN MOSELEY

I was thrilled to be the Flower Expert on **THE PATCH** because I've always had a desire to encourage more people to grow and arrange flowers. I can't remember a time when they weren't a part of my life — I even had my own little patches to grow them in both my parents' and grandparents' gardens.

SPRING BASKET TABLE ARRANGEMENT

The bright hues of bulbs look best when arranged in blocks of colour for impact. These yellow tulips offer a strong structure, and their impact is softened slightly by the silvery down of pussy willow stems and variegated foliage. When arranged in a basket, and decorated with an exuberant raffia bow plus a few quails' eggs, this makes a joyous spring arrangement that can be set on a side table to bring the first stirrings of life and colour of this season indoors.

METHOD

1. Soak enough florist's foam (see page 187) to fill the basket almost to the top, cut the flower stems at a 45-degree angle and strip off the leaves. Wire up the plastic quails' eggs (see page 187). If you can't find plastic eggs, make a small hole in each end of real ones and blow out the insides, then wire them up.

2. Line the basket with moss then soak it with water. Place the soaked florist's foam in the basket and secure in position using florist's tape.

3. Now form the basic shape of the floral design, starting with the eucalyptus and variegated ivy to create a framework. Cut each piece to length before placing it in the florist's foam.

4. Next, add the tulips. To ensure the arrangement looks good from all sides, start by placing a 'fan' of tulips in the centre of the basket along its length. Now fill the front of the basket, cutting the tulips in the front to the shortest length, making the stems progressively longer until you reach the original line. Repeat with the back.

5. Use the rest of the greenery to fill any gaps, letting the variegated ivy trail prettily.

6. Add the pussy willow to the centre, to give height to the arrangement.

7. Make a bow out of the raffia and wire it into position in the middle of the front of the basket.

Jonathan's tips
for beautiful basket arrangements

Basket arrangements lend a country feel to floral designs, and although functionally they're really just another vase, they have the perception of offering so much more, inviting you to add in extras that you might put in a basket – such as the little quails' eggs in this design.

HAND-TIED BOUQUET

The sheer variety of summer flowers can be made up into the loveliest of bouquets that catches the very essence of the season. Pick from what you have available to create an attractive combination of colours and textures, and aim to add in a little sweet-smelling something, such as sweet peas, lavender, or even rosemary. This bouquet is a glorious combination of sweet peas, zinnias and lavender with a froth of *Alchemilla mollis* (lady's mantle), and is given definition by a collar of bold, variegated hosta leaves. Everything is decoratively held together with simple raffia.

METHOD

1   Organise yourself before you get started and have only one free hand! First lay out all the flowers and foliage into sections of the same varieties and cut the string or raffia to length, ready for binding.

2   Hold the stems in one hand and feed in the flowers one at a time with the other so they spiral around a neat binding point. They should fan out at the top and bottom to create a 'waist' in the middle, which you should hold as you make the bouquet and where you will bind the finished bouquet with raffia to hold it together.

3   Each time you add stems, turn the bouquet very slightly, so you can see how it is progressing. If you're not happy with the position of a stem, relax your holding hand slightly and remove and reposition the flower.

4   Add in foliage for contrast and to support the more delicate flowers, preventing them slipping and moving around while you work. Avoid heavy or branched material – straighter-stemmed foliage works best. Use larger green leaves around the outside to give the bouquet a round shape and to accentuate the colours of the flowers.

5   Use string or raffia to tie off the bouquet, but not too tightly or you'll strangle the stems. Finally, cut the stems to the same length to create a flat base so the bouquet can stand up.

Jonathan's tips
for the best bouquets

Bouquets aren't just for summer – you can use the basic principles in any season, although outside of summer you may have fewer flowers to choose from. The key is to pick enough material to make up a generous bunch. You'll need plenty – allow for at least thirty stems.

SUMMER TABLE ARRANGEMENT

The stunning pink, purple and green palette of this table centre is created using roses, dahlias, tiny indigo asters, limey lady's mantle (Alchemilla) and bells of Ireland (Molucella). The long, low shape is made using tall flowers such as gladioli and bells of Ireland horizontally at the base and short-cut roses and dahlias to give gentle height in the centre. You don't have to restrict the arrangement to flowers and foliage; for extra interest and depth of colour, this setting includes apples, aubergines, blue-veined cabbage leaves and deep-purple beans too!

METHOD

1   Cut stems at an angle and strip off the leaves.

2   Wire up any fruits you are using (see page 187).

3   Create the rough outline with the greenery, using gladioli and mollucella horizontally to give length to the arrangement.

4   Create a definite focal centre with the tallest flowers, and the larger wired-up fruits and vegetables, then blend in complementary colours.

5   Once the main flowers are in, fill around them with supplementary flowers, foliage and the smaller wired-up fruits and vegetables.

Jonathan's tips
for top table arrangements
Long, low arrangements are the perfect solution for dining tables because anything at eye level or higher gets in the way of conversation with the person opposite you.

SUMMER WREATH

Summer wreaths make pretty celebration arrangements that can be used both indoors and out. There's a formality to wreaths that make them appropriate for special occasions, such as weddings or baby-naming celebrations. This one wittily introduces green with flowers, rather than foliage, adding zest to pink and lilac blooms. The combination of cream and lilac roses, neat chrysanthemums and dahlias, and zingy zinnias creates a compact wreath.

METHOD

1. Soak a florist's foam ring in water with added liquid plant food to keep the wreath looking good in the summer heat.

2. Using a florist's knife, or other sharp knife, cut the stems of the plant material to a point, like a quill, so that they penetrate the foam easily.

3. Shave off the hard corners of the foam into an angled corner. This gives you a greater surface area to arrange the flowers.

4. Start with the foliage to create the basic framework of the shape.

5. Once the greenery border is in place, make the hanging loop using several strands of soft garden twine tied securely around the top of the floral foam ring, avoiding the join as that is where it is weakest.

6. Begin to fill out with flowers.

7. The wreath will look different when it is hung up, so if you are working on a flat surface, keep holding the wreath upright and stand away from the design every now and then to assess its development.

8. Finally, fill any gaps with spare leaves/greenery.

9. Keep the design fresh by misting the flowers every day with a water spray.

For Jonathan's top tips for wreaths, see page 204.

HANGING FLORAL DESIGN

Hanging designs have a lavish quality – perfect for occasions with a carnival or festival feel, such as summer balls, special birthday parties or anniversaries. You can really go over the top for the sheer joy of it! This arrangement includes pink roses, cream chrysanthemums, blue hydrangeas and eryngium, burgundy trails of amaranthus, and plenty of fruit – apples, brambles and even a few baby corncobs! It's finished off with a 'tail' of rose-filled glass tubes suspended by wire from the bottom of the arrangement for a bit of over-the-top party sparkle!

METHOD

1   Put a couple of florist's foam rings back to back, which you will be able to tie rope or wire to for suspension, and soak them. Cut several long lengths of heavy-gauge florist's wire or galvanised garden wire and twist them together. Pass these through the soaked foam rings (avoid the join in the plastic as the ring is weaker there) and twist them together at the top of the rings. Take the long ends and wind them together to make a loop for hanging.

2   Now prepare the material: cut stems at an angle and strip them of leaves. Wire up any fruit you want to use (see page 187).

3   Start with the greenery to get the rough shape, letting it trail down. Next, add flowers in all directions – some high, some low, and not forgetting the middle. Repeat some larger flowers around the design to create rhythm. Flowers that have big heads on small or weak stems, such as dahlias, should be added at the end, to keep them intact.

4   Finally, add over-the-top elements such as feathers, suspended crystals or test-tubes with flowers in. Be inventive, creative and flamboyant!

Jonathan's tips
for fabulous hanging floral designs

Large hanging designs are surprisingly heavy once you have soaked florist's foam and all the plant material. Before you start, work out where you want it to hang and make sure the structure can take the finished weight. Look for the wooden door linings of double doors into a through-room, for example, or the beam in a ceiling. Fix a hook securely using butterfly fixings. If in doubt, make the design smaller and lighter.

You'll need plenty of plant material because the design has to look good from all angles – it will be seen from the sides, underneath, and, if it is to hang in a stairwell, possibly above, too. You must also cover up all the 'mechanics'. Pay attention to the even distribution of weight throughout the design. This will not only make it look good, but also ensure that it hangs straight.

TOPIARY TREE

Floral topiary trees have nursery storybook charm, perhaps because they're mimicking something other than a flower arrangement. Whatever the reason, they are very useful in floral decoration terms because you can use them in many different ways. This delightful autumn example mixes shades of orange, yellow and green through seedheads, flowers and fruits in the form of tiny green tomatoes on their vines.

METHOD

1   Three-quarters fill a terracotta pot with dry florist's foam then fill it to the top with soaked wet foam.

2   Cut the stems at a 45-degree angle, strip off the leaves and wire any fruits (see page 187).

3   Push a bunch of about six stems into the centre of the foam to make a trunk. Wire them together firmly at the top of the stems.

4   Push a soaked florist's foam ball onto the top of the trunk and use medium-gauge florist's wire to secure it into position.

5   If you are using large flowers with big stems, like these sunflowers, start with these. Shave the stem to a sharp nib and push some straight wire through the flower head and out the other side to secure it in the foam.

6   When the sunflower heads are in, fill with smaller flowers and foliage. Group flowers and other foliage to maintain the rounded shape of the topiary, then soften with smaller filler flowers. Be inventive; bundles of beans, tiny tomatoes, artichoke heads and peppers can look fabulous, and even bundles of sticks give extra texture.

7   Finally, cover the base with flowers and foliage that echo the design at the head of the topiary.

Jonathan's tips
for theatrical topiary trees

Topiary trees are delightful on their own as side arrangements, but their architectural quality also makes them ideal for adding a sense of theatre to many other situations. You could make up a pair to set either side of an entrance, or they'd also make a striking statement positioned in a row down the centre of a long table, or one in the centre of several round tables. Once guests are seated, the main floral orb will be well above eye level, so it won't hinder conversation.

PEDESTAL

Where you need to create impact from a distance, use a pedestal arrangement. Typically, these are used in larger venues at a wedding, baby naming ceremony, or at presentations or formal functions. The idea is to create height so the flowers can be seen from the back of the room. This fabulous autumn arrangement, set on an old milk churn, features big, bold sunflowers, dahlias, hydrangeas and zinnias which provide rounded shapes set against tall, upright gladioli and corn on the cob, softened by trailing amaranthus flowers.

METHOD

1. Start by building the structure. Using florist's tape, secure a large, soaked obelisk of florist's foam in a tray of water. If you can't find an obelisk, make your own using blocks of florist's foam piled on top of each other and secured with tape or wire. Set the tray on a firm surface while you work – you will move it to the pedestal once it's finished.

2. Cut the stems at a 45-degree angle and strip the stems of leaves. Start building the shape of the floral design using foliage. Use a balance of weighty pieces of foliage all around, including the back of the design as this helps with the balance and stops it toppling over.

3. As you use the foliage and, later, the flowers, concentrate on creating height by using long upright stems, such as gladioli. Let longer, trailing foliage and flowers such as amaranthus hang down over the tray.

4. Use larger blooms to accentuate the central line downwards and select large weighty flowers to establish a focal area. Chrysanthemums can look very blocky, so split up the sprays, and chop a few flowers out of the multi-headed sprays to allow light and air between the blooms.

5. As you arrange the flowers, turn some to face towards the back to show their profile and use interesting textures of foliage flowers, seedheads, berries, fruits and vegetables to create impact and individuality and to evenly balance the arrangement and fill gaps.

Jonathan's tips
for a perfect pedestal
Take a tip from theatre designers when creating pedestal arrangements: they are meant to be seen from afar, so, whatever the season, don't try to be subtle. Make bold statements with colours and shapes, grouping flowers if necessary for extra definition. While you're working, step back every now and then and stand a few metres away from the arrangement to check the strength of the design.

CHRISTMAS WREATH

The success of this wreath is that while it keeps to the traditional red and green Christmas colour scheme, there's lots of variety in each of the colours. The greens range from blue fir to the lightest and most delicate variegated ivy and deep green holly leaves edged with yellow. The greens are further brightened with the merry orb-like ivy fruits. Try to get as many lighter tones into Christmas door wreaths as possible, otherwise they disappear into darkness as the night draws in.

METHOD

1. Soak a florist's foam ring in water with added liquid plant food to keep the wreath looking good all through the Christmas break.

2. Using a florist's knife, or other sharp knife, cut the stems of the plant material to a point, like a quill, so that they penetrate the oasis easily.

3. Shave off the hard corners of the ring into an angled corner to give you a greater surface area to arrange the flowers.

4. Start with the foliage to create the basic framework of the shape.

5. Once the greenery border is in place, make the hanging loop using several strands of soft garden twine tied securely around the top of the floral foam ring, avoiding the join as that is where it is weakest.

6. Begin to fill out with flowers, arranging them so that they are evenly distributed.

7. Your wreath design will look different when it is hung up, so if you are working on a flat surface, keep holding it upright and stand away from the design every now and then to assess its development.

8. Finally, fill any gaps with spare leaves/greenery.

9. Keep the design fresh by misting the flowers every day with a water spray.

Jonathan's tips for wonderful winter wreaths

Whether you're making a wreath for Christmas or any other time of the year, aim to make a balanced design. Do this either by mixing the focus materials (flowers or berries) evenly around the wreath, or by making special focus clusters and repeating them several times around the wreath. It's always good to use an odd number of these, so aim for five clusters or, if your wreath is very large, you may like to use seven.

Eat

There's something deeply and fundamentally satisfying about eating food that you have grown yourself. You can harvest it when it is perfectly ready, sun ripened and bursting with flavour, to be eaten immediately before any of its nutrients have started to diminish.

By contrast, fruit or vegetables you buy will have been transported to and stored by the supermarket or greengrocer, and all the time will be using up their own nutrients from the moment they were cut from the plant, which was their food source. That process is accelerated immediately you cut into the fruit or vegetable. So instead of buying ready prepared cut salads, you can claim all the nutrients yourself by wandering down into the garden and gathering exactly what you want to serve fresh at the next meal.

Having said that, there are times when the garden is so abundant that it can be difficult to keep up. The race is then on to capture the goodness, and store it for later in the year when that crop is no longer available. From midsummer onwards, you can use up gluts in delicious homemade summer fruit jams and curds and bottle up berries in cordials, but it's autumn, the harvest season, when you will be at your busiest. Traditionally, this was the time of year when everyone devoted many hours to making autumn jams, chutneys and pickles. Fruits and vegetables were also canned, or bottled into large glass jars, the precursors of our cans today. All these delicious preserves were stored to last through the winter months, bringing sweet condiments, vibrant flavours and essential nutrients to what was often a limited seasonal diet. Nowadays, homemade preserves are still seen as treats and make wonderful gifts for friends or neighbours, especially if you package them up in lovely jars.

PRESERVING EQUIPMENT

There are just a few pieces of specialist preserving equipment that are worth investing in.

Jam preserving pans are large and wide, designed to speed the reducing process. They have gradations marked on the inside for measuring quantities, a pouring lip and handle to lift the heavy pan. These large pans have sloping sides; their size and design allows the mixture plenty of room to come up to a rolling boil, and speeds up the evaporation and therefore reduction of the mixture. Stainless steel is a good choice as it is vinegar-proof. You can make do with any heavy bottomed stainless-steel pan, but choose a wide one.

Cooking thermometers are used to measure the temperature for the setting point of your preserve and water temperatures for bottling.

Jam funnels aid the speedy filling of the jars – essential when you're working with hot liquid.

Jam-jar tongs are good both for safely taking sterilised jars out of the oven and lifting lids from boiling water.

Jelly bags allow juice to be strained from cooked fruit. Set over a bowl and left for several hours, the resulting juice will then be clear and ready for use.

Jars and lids are an inexpensive way to package preserves. Choose vinegar-proof plastic-lined lids, essential for making chutneys and pickles. Lids are available separately, if you want to recycle old jars.

Preserving jars are generally more robust than basic jars and are available either with screw tops or with lids and seals, which are held in place with clips. These aid the sealing process because when the hot liquid is put into the hot jar and sealed, the metal clip expands just enough for any trapped air to escape, but contracts as it cools, forming a tight seal. You can test the seal by unclipping and lifting up the jar by its lid. It should remain sealed. To open, pull the tab on the seal upwards. Seals that have not deteriorated or damaged can be re-used. Otherwise, buy new each year.

STERILISING

Jars must be properly sterilised, otherwise mould, yeasts and bacteria could infect the preserve. Some sources say you can do this in the dishwasher, but this is risky as the hottest cycle in many appliances is only 60°C (140°F), whereas some moulds and fungi can survive temperatures of up to almost 100°C (212°F). To avoid cracking, the jars need to be the same temperature as the preserve when they are filled. Here's the method:

1   Thoroughly check the jars, lids and seals and discard any that are damaged.
2   Heat the oven to 180°C (356°F) and while it is heating, scrub out the jars, their lids and seals in warm soapy water. Drain.
3   Arrange the jars on an oven tray so they are not touching and put them into the oven for at least 10 minutes. Meanwhile, boil the lids and seals for 10 minutes.
4   When you are ready to fill the jars, use tongs to take them out of the oven and put on a heatproof surface. Remove the lids and seals from the boiling water.

FILLING AND SEALING

Fill the jars to within 6mm (¼in) of the top then wipe clean the rim and either screw on the lid or, if you have preserving jars, put the seals on the lids, seal and close the jar.

Alternatively, place a wax disc, wax side down, on the surface of the jam, then use a cellophane cover. This should be moistened then secured with elastic bands. As they dry, they shrink to create an airtight seal. The jars should be sealed immediately while the contents are still very hot.

PRESERVING METHODS

Here are some traditional preserving methods.

Jam is made by combining fresh fruit and sugar and boiling them together until the 'setting point' is reached. The setting point depends on the combination of the sugar and the pectin and acid in the fruit. Different fruits have different amounts of pectin. Recipes for fruits that are naturally low in pectin and acid will need these added. For this you can use lemon juice and commercial pectin. Preserving sugar is the best to use for jams as it dissolves quickly.

Jelly is bright, clear and has a softer set than jam. Once the fruit is cooked, it needs to drip into a bowl through a jelly bag. This can take many hours, and is best left overnight. Don't be tempted to squeeze the bag or press the fruit through as this will cloud the jelly.

Cordials and syrups are made from fresh fruits that are boiled with sugar and strained through a jelly bag overnight. Once bottled, they are further preserved by putting them on a trivet in a deep pan filled with water to within 2.5cm (1in) of the top of the bottle. The water is brought to a simmer and held there for twenty minutes.

Curds are soft spreads made with eggs, so they don't have a long shelf life and should be stored in the fridge and used within a month.

Chutney is a savoury condiment made of fruit or vegetables mixed with spices and sugar and cooked in vinegar. Chutneys are often left for several months to mature before they are eaten.

Pickles are fresh fruit or vegetables that are often prepared by brining or dry salting, and then preserved in vinegar.

Bottling is a traditional way to preserve fruit and vegetables. It is a time-consuming process that involves packing ingredients into jars and covering them with syrup or brine. The jars are then sealed and processed in a water bath. There are three quick, modern equivalent recipes from page 248.

Meet the Expert

THANE PRINCE

I'm so excited and thrilled to be the Eat Expert for THE PATCH. From the moment I saw the allotments I yearned for one! They reminded me of the veg patch my parents had in Norfolk, where I grew up. We used to harvest the fruits and vegetables and also pick blackberries from the hedgerows, then my mother, my sisters and I would make them up into delicious jams and pickles.

I think the desire to preserve food and be able to store it is intrinsic to us, going back to the earliest times – it's deep in our DNA. Through history preserving has been an essential part of survival. These days, people like to make a connection with what they're eating; they want to know what's in their food. If you make something yourself, you choose what's going into it. There might be lots of sugar in jam, for example, but if you love jam and have seen how much sugar it needs, you might just eat a small amount. I love food and enjoy eating almost anything, especially when I know how it was grown and what it contains.

Preserves provide a point of interest in a meal and there are so many new flavours to add. The English have always shamelessly plundered ideas from other cultures. We might add chillies and piquant ingredients from the Far East to our pickles now, but that's not so different from mango chutney, which was exotic in Victorian times, or the olives brought to us by the Romans.

I was looking for preserves from the allotmenteers that would excite the palate, and was delighted by the recipes they came up with. The breadth of ideas was extraordinary when you think they were limited to crops they could grow in just four months. The recipes included here are the ones that really stood out for me as both innovative and exciting on the programme.

PETALBERRY JAM <A RECIPE FROM THE PATCH>

Jams

Here's a basic strawberry jam given a twist with rosewater and scented rose petals that can be made from your own fruit and flower harvest. The delightful perfumed flavour is perfect for tea and scones in the summer rose garden! If you prefer a more standard strawberry jam, just leave out the rosewater and petals.

INGREDIENTS

400g strawberries
juice of 1 lemon
400g jam sugar with added pectin
1 large perfumed rose
2 tsp rosewater

METHOD

1   Hull the strawberries and cut any large ones in half. Place in a preserving pan with the lemon juice and cook gently over a low heat for about 20 minutes, breaking them up with a fork or potato masher. Meanwhile, place two saucers in the freezer to chill.

2   Add the sugar and heat gently, stirring, until dissolved.

3   Bring to the boil and cook rapidly for about 5 minutes or until setting point is reached. This may take up to 20 minutes. Test for the setting point by removing the saucers from the freezer and dropping a teaspoonful of jam onto it. Chill for a couple of minutes (removing the jam from the heat to prevent over cooking), then push your finger through the jam – it should wrinkle and feel thick; if not, boil again for a couple more minutes.

4   Remove the petals from the rose and stir into the jam with the rosewater and cook for 2 minutes.

5   Remove any scum from the jam with a slotted spoon. Pour into clean sterilised jars and seal with sterilised lids.

MAKES 2 x 500g JARS

BASIC RASPBERRY JAM

The classic teatime favourite, fresh and fruity raspberry jam is delicious spread on hot buttered toast or scones or used to sandwich layers of a traditional Victoria sponge cake. If you have summer- and autumn-fruiting raspberries (see page 152), you can be making this jam right through a long season.

INGREDIENTS
1kg raspberries
juice of 1 lemon
1kg granulated sugar

METHOD

1   Place the raspberries in a preserving pan and add the lemon juice. Cook for 5 minutes until the berries have reduced to a pulp.

2   Add the sugar and heat gently, stirring until the sugar has dissolved.

3   Bring the mixture to the boil and boil rapidly for 5 minutes or until setting point has been reached (see page 213).

4   Remove any scum from the jam with a slotted spoon. Pour into clean sterilised jars and seal with sterilised lids.

MAKES 3–4 x 500g JARS

BASIC BLACKCURRANT JAM

Blackcurrant jam has a slightly sharp aftertaste but a fresh flavour. The fruit is a jam-maker's favourite because it is naturally high in pectin, the setting agent, making the recipe foolproof. Let the glossy black berries smother the plant to get enough for this jam.

INGREDIENTS

1kg blackcurrants
1.5kg granulated sugar

METHOD

1 Run a fork down the strig to remove the blackcurrants from their stems. Place the fruit in a large pan with 750ml cold water, bring to the boil, then simmer until the currants are tender and the mixture has reduced considerably. As the pulp thickens, stir frequently to prevent burning.

2 Add the sugar, heat gently and stir until it has dissolved, then boil hard for 5 minutes or until the jam reaches setting point (see page 213).

3 Pour into clean sterilised jars and seal with sterilised lids.

MAKES 5 x 500g JARS

BLACKBERRY AND APPLE JAM

In September, the hedgerows are laden with ripe blackberries bursting with flavour and ready for harvest. Team these with windfalls of cooking apples to make delicious fruity jam which you can enjoy all through the winter.

INGREDIENTS

1kg blackberries
500g cooking apples,
  peeled, cored and
  roughly diced
1.5kg granulated sugar

METHOD

1 Place the blackberries and apples in a preserving pan or large saucepan with 150ml water and cook for 5–10 minutes until the fruit is soft and tender.

2 Add the sugar and stir until it is dissolved, then boil for 10 minutes or until setting point is reached (see page 213). Remove any scum with a slotted spoon.

3 Allow to cool for 5 minutes to prevent the fruit rising to the surface, then pour into clean sterilised jars, filling right to the top. Seal with sterilised lids.

MAKES 5 x 500g JARS

AUBERGINE AND MUSTARD PICKLE

If you garden in a warm, sunny spot or have a greenhouse, you could try growing aubergines (page 111) and then preserve them in this truly wonderful pickle. The mellow combination of flavours in this spicy pickle is surprising and a brilliant way to use up any aubergines that are past their best. A delectable dip for poppadums and naan breads, it's delicious with curries and can also be used to give a Middle Eastern twist to cold lamb.

INGREDIENTS

3 large aubergines (about 1kg)

2 tbsp salt

2 tsp cumin seeds

2 tsp coriander seeds

5 tbsp vegetable oil

2 onions, peeled and finely chopped

4 cloves garlic, crushed

3 red chillies, deseeded and finely chopped

50g fresh root ginger, grated

2 tsp yellow mustard seeds

2 tbsp tamarind paste

150g granulated sugar

200ml white vinegar

METHOD

1   Quarter the aubergines lengthwise then cut into 3cm cubes. Place in a colander and sprinkle with salt. Leave for 1 hour then rinse and pat dry with kitchen paper.

2   Place the cumin and coriander seeds in a small pan and dry-fry for a minute or so until the aromas are released, then grind them to a powder.

3   Heat 3 tablespoons of oil in a frying pan and fry the aubergines until just browned. Transfer to a large pan, then add the remaining oil to the frying pan and fry the onions for 5 minutes until softened. Add the garlic, chillies, ginger, mustard seeds and ground spices and cook for another couple of minutes, then add to the large pan with the aubergines.

4   Stir in the tamarind paste, sugar and vinegar and cook gently until the sugar has dissolved. Bring to the boil, then reduce the heat and simmer for about 40 minutes until the mixture is thick.

5   Pour into clean sterilised jars and seal with vinegar-proof lids. This will keep for up to a year unopened.

MAKES 3 x 500g JARS

BLUEBERRY CURD <A RECIPE FROM THE PATCH>

The amazing colour of this curd is matched by its delicious taste. The surprising addition of coriander enhances the flavour of the blueberries. These plants are perfect for growing in pots, as they thrive in ericacous soil which is more easily provided in containers (see page 147). Try this exotic curd spread onto warm American pancakes or scones.

INGREDIENTS
400g blueberries
6 coriander seeds
4 eggs, beaten
2 egg yolks, beaten
100g unsalted butter
200g caster sugar

METHOD

1   Place the blueberries in a medium pan with 2 tablespoons water and cook over a gentle heat until the berries burst and are softened. Meanwhile, grind the coriander seeds to a powder. Add to the blueberries and cook for 2 minutes.

2   Tip the blueberries into a fine sieve set over a bowl, then measure out 200ml of the collected juice.

3   Strain the eggs and yolks through a clean sieve and cut the butter into small cubes.

4   Place a heatproof mixing bowl over a pan of gently simmering water (the bowl should not touch the water). Place the blueberry juice into the bowl, add the butter and sugar and cook until the butter has melted. Stirring constantly, gradually pour the strained eggs into the mixture and cook until the curd has thickened enough to coat the back of a wooden spoon, and leave a slight trail in the mixture.

5   Remove from the heat, pour into a sterilised jar and seal with a sterilised lid. Store in the fridge and use within 2 weeks.

MAKES 1 x 500g JAR

REDBARB CORDIAL <A RECIPE FROM THE PATCH>

Use the last rhubarb pickings with the first redcurrants to make this sophisticated, refreshing cordial. Try it topped up with sparkling water, or add a drop to some Prosecco for a smart summer cocktail.

INGREDIENTS

450g rhubarb (use the pinkest part of the stems if possible), cut into 3cm chunks
150g redcurrants
225g caster sugar
½ tsp vanilla extract

METHOD

1 Put the rhubarb in a large pan. Run a fork down the strigs of redcurrants and place the berries in the pan with 300ml water. Bring to the boil and cook for 10 minutes until the rhubarb has reduced to a pulp.

2 Set a jelly bag or a sieve lined with muslin over a bowl. Add the fruit and let it drain for an hour. Do not press down on the fruit or the juice will become cloudy.

3 Pour the juice into a pan and stir in the sugar. Heat gently, stirring until dissolved, then bring to the boil. Add the vanilla, then pour into a sterilised bottle and seal. Cool, store in the fridge and use within a month.

MAKES ABOUT 500ml

CURRANTY CORDIAL <A RECIPE FROM THE PATCH>

This sweet, refreshing cordial makes a delicious summer drink.
Pour a little over ice in a tall glass and top up with ice-cold water.

INGREDIENTS

225g redcurrants
225g blackcurrants
150g strawberries, hulled and quartered
juice of ½ lemon
250g granulated sugar

METHOD

1 Run a fork down the strigs of currants and place the berries in a pan with the strawberries. Add 250ml water and the lemon juice, bring to the boil then simmer for 20 minutes until the fruit is tender.

2 Set a jelly bag or a sieve lined with muslin over a bowl. Add the fruit and let it drain for at least 30 minutes. Do not press down on the fruit or the juice will become cloudy.

3 Place the juice in a pan, stir in the sugar and boil for 5 minutes. Transfer to a sterilised bottle and seal. Cool, store in the fridge and use within a month.

MAKES ABOUT 300ML

APPLE AND GINGER CORDIAL

Use up garden apples and add spicy ginger to make this warming yet refreshing autumn cordial. Top up a little cordial with ice-cold water and serve with ice cubes and perhaps a sprig of homegrown mint, if you like.

INGREDIENTS

1kg eating apples, peeled, quartered and cores removed
25g fresh root ginger, sliced
375g granulated sugar

METHOD

1   Place the apples in a large pan with 300ml water and the ginger. Cook for 15–20 minutes or until the apples have become soft and pulpy.

2   Set a jelly bag or a sieve lined with muslin over a bowl. Add the fruit and let it drain for at least 30 minutes. Do not press down on the fruit or the juice will become cloudy.

3   Measure the juice and add 375g sugar for every 600ml of juice. Place in a pan and boil for 5 minutes.

4   Pour into sterilised bottles and seal tightly. Cool, store in the fridge and use within a month.

MAKES 1 x 500ml BOTTLE

TOMATO CHUTNEY

Tomatoes are easy and satisfying to grow (see page 134). If you're inundated with fruits, turn some into a delicious chutney you can enjoy when summer is over. This is the perfect sweet-sour chutney for burgers, hot dogs or just a chunk of cheese.

INGREDIENTS

2kg ripe tomatoes
1kg onions, finely chopped
1 clove garlic, crushed
100g sultanas
250g cooking apples, cored and roughly chopped
300g granulated sugar
225ml cider vinegar
2 tsp salt
½ tsp ground ginger
1 tsp paprika
½ tsp dried chilli flakes

METHOD

1 Cut a cross in each tomato then place in a bowl and cover with boiling water. Leave for 1–2 minutes, then drain and place in cold water. Peel away the skins.

2 Roughly chop the tomatoes and place in a preserving pan with the remaining ingredients. Bring to the boil.

3 Reduce the heat and simmer for 1¼–1½ hours or until the chutney has a thick pulpy consistency.

4 Pour into clean sterilised jars and cover with vinegar-proof lids. Store for at least 2 weeks before serving. This will keep for up to 1 year unopened.

MAKES 5–6 x 500g JARS

GREEN TOMATO CHUTNEY

As autumn arrives, any green tomatoes left on the vine are unlikely to ripen before the frost. But harvest them anyway and combine them with cooking apples and onions to create a delicious green tomato chutney.

INGREDIENTS

1kg green tomatoes
500g onions, finely chopped
500g cooking apples, peeled, cored and chopped
100g raisins
1 clove garlic, crushed
1 tsp ground ginger
pinch ground cloves
250g light muscovado sugar
300ml malt vinegar

METHOD

1 Place all the ingredients in a preserving pan and bring to the boil. Reduce the heat and simmer for 1¼–1½ hours or until the chutney has reached a thick pulpy consistency.

2 Pour into clean sterilised jars and cover with vinegar-proof lids. Store for at least 2 weeks before serving. This will keep for up to 1 year unopened.

MAKES ABOUT 3 x 500g JARS

QUICKALILLI

This favourite garden pickle started off as the English interpretation of traditional Indian relishes. Packed with vegetables, it's a great way to use up all the odds and ends of your harvest, and is easily adapted to whatever surpluses you might have. Its sweet and mustardy flavour makes it brilliant for livening up roast ham, a ham sandwich or a cheese ploughman's.

INGREDIENTS

Choose from any of these 5 or 6 types of
   vegetable, to total 1kg prepared weight:
   Radishes, sliced
   Cucumber, deseeded and diced
   Courgettes, sliced
   Peppers, deseeded and chopped
   Shallots, sliced
   Cauliflower, broken into small florets
   Runner beans, sliced
   French beans, trimmed and chopped
50g salt

FOR THE SAUCE

600ml cider vinegar
30g cornflour
10g ground turmeric
10g English mustard powder
40g fresh root ginger, grated
3 tsp mustard seeds
1 tsp cumin seeds
1 tsp coriander seeds
150g caster sugar

METHOD

1. Prepare all the vegetables then place them in a colander over a bowl. Sprinkle with salt and stir well. Leave for 12–24 hours then drain, rinse well and drain again.

2. Measure 100ml vinegar into a small bowl, add the cornflour, turmeric and mustard powder and set aside.

3. For the sauce, place the remaining vinegar, ginger and spices in a large pan with the sugar and bring to the boil. Add all the vegetables and cook for 5 minutes.

4. Stir the cornflour mixture and pour into the boiling mixture, stir well and cook for a further 2 minutes until thickened.

5. Pour into sterilised jars, seal and store for up to 6 months, unopened.

MAKES 1–1½ LITRES

ALLOTMENT CHUTNEY

This delicious sweet chutney makes use of the easy to grow favourites that might feature in your patch. A few dried chillies have been added to this recipe to give it a bit of a kick, but if you like a sweeter pickle, just leave them out.

INGREDIENTS

250g carrots
350g swede
1 small cauliflower
2 onions, peeled
2 courgettes
250g raw beetroot
3 large cooking apples, peeled
125g raisins
4 cloves garlic, crushed

250g molasses sugar
1 tsp salt
4 tbsp lemon juice
350ml malt vinegar
1 tbsp Worcestershire sauce
2 tsp yellow mustard seeds
2 tsp crushed dried chillies (optional)
2 tsp ground allspice
2 tbsp cornflour

METHOD

1   Dice the vegetables and apples into small chunks and place them in a preserving pan with all the remaining ingredients except the cornflour. Bring to the boil then reduce the heat and simmer the mixture for 1 hour until the vegetables are tender but retain some bite. The liquid will have reduced by half but the mixture should still be a little wet.

2   Mix the cornflour with a little cold water then stir into the chutney and bring to the boil. Cook for 2–3 minutes until thickened and the mixture does not taste floury.

3   Pour the pickle into hot sterilised jars, cover with a vinegar-proof lid and screw the lid on loosely. Allow to cool, then tighten the lids and store in a cool cupboard. The pickle should be left for at least a month to allow the flavours to develop before using. The chutney will keep for up to 1 year, unopened.

MAKES 4 x 500g JARS

CURRIED CARROT CHUTNEY

A RECIPE FROM THE PATCH Carrots are a great crop for raised beds or containers and with successive sowing you could be eating them for much of the year. If you grow too many, use them up with some onions in a batch of this delicious, richly spiced chutney with an Indian flavour. Pour it into lots of small jars to give away or sell at school or village fairs.

INGREDIENTS

3 tbsp olive oil
3 large onions, peeled and finely chopped
1.2kg carrots, cut into dice
7.5cm piece fresh root ginger
3 cloves garlic
3 large red chillies, finely chopped
1 tbsp ground cumin
1 tbsp ground coriander
1 tbsp ground turmeric
good shake of salt and ground black pepper
600g muscovado sugar
1.2 litres cider vinegar
25g coriander leaves

METHOD

1   Heat the oil in a large pan and fry the onions for 5–6 minutes until softened but not browned. Add the carrots and 9 tablespoons cold water. Place a lid on the pan and cook over a medium heat for 10 minutes until the carrots are just tender when pierced with a knife.

2   Peel and finely chop the ginger and garlic and stir into the carrots. Cook for 1 minute then add the chillies, spices, seasoning, sugar and vinegar. Bring back to the boil and boil gently for 20–30 minutes until the liquid is reduced by two-thirds and the mixture is thick.

3   Remove the chutney from the heat and stir in the coriander. Bring to the boil and boil for 2 minutes.

4   Pour the chutney into clean sterilised jars, cover with a vinegar-proof lid and secure lightly. When cold, tighten the lids and leave in a cool dark place for at least 1 month before using. This will keep for 6 months, unopened.

MAKES 5–6 x 250ml JARS

Relishes

BEETROOT RELISH

Beetroots are easy to grow (see page 114) and can be used in this delicious earthy yet sweet relish. Brilliant with roast beef or in a cold roast beef sandwich, or served on toasts with grilled goat's cheese.

INGREDIENTS

300g raw beetroot
½ large onion
2 tsp olive oil
½ tsp yellow mustard seeds
110ml balsamic vinegar
110ml white wine vinegar
210g caster sugar
1 clove
pinch sea salt and ground black pepper

METHOD

1   Peel the beetroot (you might want to wear disposable gloves or washing-up gloves to avoid staining your hands) and onion, then chop roughly and place in a food processor. Blend until finely chopped.

2   Heat the olive oil in a large frying pan and then add the mustard seeds, cook for a few seconds with the pan lid on until you hear them pop, then add all the remaining ingredients and 110ml water.

3   Bring to the boil, then cover and simmer for about 30 minutes or until the beetroot is soft and the liquid has reduced to make a thick relish.

4   Pour into a clean sterilised jar and seal with a vinegar-proof lid. This will keep for up to 6 months unopened. Once opened, keep in the fridge.

MAKES 1 x 300g JAR

CABALLERO SALSA A RECIPE FROM THE PATCH

This deliciously hot and spicy tomato-based relish goes well with cheese and Mexican foods, or use it instead of ordinary ketchup to liven up everyday meals. This makes great use of summer's most juicy tomatoes, and perhaps even some homegrown chillies (see page 117).

INGREDIENTS

4 large ripe tomatoes
1 onion, peeled and diced
1½ tbsp sea salt
250ml white wine vinegar
3 or 4 black chillies (or use red if not available)
4 cloves garlic
200g caster sugar
1 tbsp coriander seeds
2 tsp cayenne pepper
2 tsp cumin seeds, crushed
15g fresh coriander, chopped

METHOD

1 Cut a cross in each tomato then place in a bowl and cover with boiling water. Leave for 1–2 minutes, then drain and place in cold water. Peel away the skins. Chop the tomatoes and place in a glass bowl with the onion and sprinkle with the salt. Cover and leave overnight.

2 Drain the liquid from the tomatoes. Place the tomato and onions in a medium pan with the vinegar and bring to the boil. Cook for 5 minutes then add the remaining ingredients except the coriander. Simmer for 30–40 minutes until most of the liquid has been reduced and the mixture has thickened.

3 Using a hand blender, purée the mixture slightly, but not completely as you still want it to be chunky.

4 Add the coriander and boil for 2 minutes. Cool, then pour into a hot sterilised jar and seal tightly with a lid.

MAKES ABOUT 1 x 300g JAR

FENNEL RELISH

The zesty aniseed and lemon flavour of this relish is a quick and easy way to turn simple grilled or poached fish into a fresh, flavoursome summer dish. Fennel has a delicious tang in recipes and its stately, feathery fronds make a beautiful focal point in any garden (see page 139).

INGREDIENTS

2 medium fennel bulbs
1 medium onion, peeled
450ml cider vinegar
115g caster sugar
large pinch salt
1 tbsp fennel seeds
15g bunch parsley
zest and juice of 1 lemon

METHOD

1. Trim off the tough stalks of the fennel then grate the fennel bulb and onion coarsely (use the grating blade of a food processor if you have one). Place the fennel and onion in a medium pan with all the remaining ingredients except the lemon zest.

2. Bring to the boil then simmer for a few minutes until some of the liquid has evaporated to leave a thick relish.

3. Add the lemon zest to the mixture.

4. Pour into a sterilised jar and seal with a vinegar-proof lid. Keep in the fridge for up to one month. Once opened, use within one week.

MAKES 1 x 550ml JAR

GARCIA'S GREEN SAUCE

Here's a great way to preserve the chilli harvest. This hot sauce makes a great dip for tortilla chips, or can be used to quickly give a bit of a kick to simple mince recipes.

INGREDIENTS

3 large green peppers
1 tbsp olive oil
1 medium onion, peeled and diced
2 green chillies (we used Big Devil)
5 yellow chillies (we used Lemon Drop)
4 cloves garlic, crushed
1½ tsp sea salt
250ml white wine vinegar

METHOD

1. Heat the oven to 200°C, 180°C Fan, Gas 6. Cut the peppers in half, remove the seeds and core and place the peppers skin side up on a baking tray. Roast for 20–30 minutes until the skin is browned and blistered. Place in a plastic bag and leave to cool a little. The steam will help the skins to peel off easily. Peel and chop the peppers.

2. Heat the oil in a medium-sized pan and fry the onion for 5 minutes until softened but not browned. Meanwhile, deseed and chop the green chillies, then chop the yellow chillies (the seeds are milder in these so there is no need to remove them). Add the garlic and chillies to the pan and cook for 1 minute.

3. Add 200ml water and the salt and cook for 20 minutes until everything is tender.

4. Using a hand blender, purée the mixture, adding the white wine vinegar a little at a time until the mixture is smooth and thick.

5. Pour into sterilised bottles and seal tightly.

6. Immerse the sealed bottle in a deep pan of boiling water so that the water reaches the top of the bottles. Bring to the boil, then simmer for 20 minutes. Drain and cool. This will keep for up to a year in the fridge.

MAKES 2 x 300ml BOTTLES

Jellies

CRAB APPLE JELLY

Crab apple trees are popular, pretty garden trees but their tiny apples are far too sour to eat. The traditional cottage-gardener's solution is to make them into the most fragrant jelly which is delicious served with roast pork.

INGREDIENTS
2kg crab apples
500g granulated sugar
juice of ½ lemon

METHOD

1   Place the crab apples in a medium pan and pour over enough water to just cover the fruit. Bring to the boil, then reduce the heat and simmer for about 20 minutes until the fruit is tender and pulpy.

2   Place a jelly bag or a sieve lined with muslin over a bowl and strain the fruit through the bag for about 8 hours or overnight. Do not press down on the fruit or it will cloud the jelly.

3   Pour the juice into a pan with the sugar. Add the lemon juice then heat gently, stirring, until the sugar has dissolved. Bring to the boil and cook at a rolling boil for 35–40 minutes, skimming off any froth that forms on top until the setting point is reached (see page 213).

4   Pour the jelly into clean sterilised jars and seal with sterilised lids. The jelly will keep for up to 6 months, unopened.

MAKES ABOUT 6 x 250g JARS

BRAMLEY APPLE AND CHILLI JELLY

This is the perfect way to use up apples in a fabulous marriage of flavours. The jelly is both sweet and hot and is delicious stirred into Thai dishes, used as a dip or even stirred into sour cream to serve with roast potatoes!

INGREDIENTS

1kg Bramley apples
100ml cider vinegar
450g granulated sugar
3 red chillies

METHOD

1 Roughly chop the whole apples – peel, pips and all. Place in a large pan with just enough water to cover the apples. Bring to the boil, then cover with a lid and simmer for about 20 minutes until the apples have become a thick pulp. Add the cider vinegar and cook for 5 minutes.

2 Place a jelly bag or a sieve lined with muslin over a bowl and strain the fruit through the bag for at least 8 hours or overnight. Do not press down on the fruit or the jelly will be cloudy.

3 Measure out the collected apple juice and pour 550ml into a large saucepan with the sugar. Heat gently, stirring, until the sugar dissolves.

4 Finely chop the chillies, removing the seeds if liked. Add to the apple mixture and boil rapidly for 10–15 minutes until setting point is reached (see page 213).

5 Pour into clean sterilised jars, cover loosely with a screw-top lid and leave to set. Then tighten the lids and store for up to 6 months.

MAKES 500ML

MINT JELLY

Mint is so easy to grow and really prolific! Add handfuls of mint to homegrown apples to make this aromatic jelly which is a fresh and delicious accompaniment to roast lamb or lamb chops.

INGREDIENTS

1kg cooking apples
15g bunch mint
600ml cider vinegar
600g granulated sugar

METHOD

1   Cut the whole apples, including the peel and cores, into small chunks. Place in a medium pan with 600ml water and 3–4 sprigs of mint. Bring to the boil then simmer gently for about 20 minutes until the apples have become a soft pulp.

2   Add the vinegar to the pan and bring to the boil. Cook for 5 minutes.

3   Place a jelly bag or a sieve lined with muslin over a bowl and strain the fruit through the bag for 6–8 hours or overnight. Do not press down on the fruit or the jelly will be cloudy.

4   Measure the juice – you should have about 750ml. Pour this into a pan with the sugar. Heat gently, stirring, until the sugar has dissolved, then boil rapidly for about 10 minutes until setting point has been reached (see page 213).

5   Chop the remaining mint and stir into the jelly. Bring to the boil and cook for 2 minutes. Pour into clean sterilised jars and seal. The jelly will keep for up to 6 months, unopened.

MAKES ABOUT 4 x 250g JARS

Bottled

PRESERVED ARTICHOKES

A RECIPE FROM THE PATCH Look for tender baby artichokes to make this preserve, as the larger ones are too tough – or better still, grow your own. Delicious served as antipasti with a platter of cold meats and cheeses.

INGREDIENTS

1 lemon, cut in half
12–14 small Petit Violet Artichokes
350ml white wine vinegar
1 bulb of garlic
Sea salt
1 tbsp black peppercorns
500ml extra virgin olive oil
5 bay leaves
1 tbsp fresh oregano leaves
herbs from the garden

METHOD

1   Squeeze the lemon juice into a large bowl of cold water, then toss in the squeezed lemon halves. Peel the tough outer stems of the artichokes to reach the tender, pale green leaves. Using a paring knife, trim the base and stem. Using a very sharp knife, trim the top, cutting off the spiky part of the leaves. Drop each artichoke in the lemony water to prevent them turning brown.

2   Heat the vinegar and 350ml water in a large pan and bring to the boil, then add the artichokes, ensuring they are completely immersed (if not, add a small pan lid to weigh them down). Simmer for 10–12 minutes until tender when pierced with a knife. Drain in a colander then squeeze out as much water as possible (wear rubber gloves to do this).

3   Break the garlic bulb into cloves and lightly crush two by pressing down on it until it splits. Place the garlic in a pan with the herbs, olive oil and seasoning. Heat gently for 5 minutes until hot but not boiling.

4   Tightly pack the artichokes into a clean sterilised jar to prevent gaps, then pour over the infused oil. Add the garlic and bay. Leave for 30 minutes then top up with more oil if necessary until the jar is full. Add the rubber seal and lid and secure tightly. Allow to cool, then store in a dark place for up to 6 months. Once opened, store in the fridge and use within 2 weeks, keeping the artichokes covered by the oil.

FILLS 1 x 1-LITRE JAR

PRESERVED COURGETTES

A RECIPE FROM THE PATCH Courgettes are one of the most prolific vegetables to grow on your vegetable patch: the more you pick, the more appear. Here's another way to enjoy them, preserved, ready to add to salads, to serve with poached salmon or to top off a delicious beef burger.

INGREDIENTS

4–8 courgettes, depending on size
50g salt
250ml white wine vinegar
2 cloves garlic, chopped
½ red chilli, deseeded and finely diced
1 tbsp salt
2 tsp dill seeds
2 tsp black peppercorns
2 tsp coriander seeds
2 tsp mustard seeds

METHOD

1   Wash the courgettes and pat dry with kitchen paper. Cut each one lengthways into very thin slices, ideally using a mandolin. Place in a large bowl and sprinkle with the salt. Cover with 120ml water and leave for 2 hours, then drain well. Pack the courgettes in strips into a large, clean sterilised jar. Alternatively, you can roll up each slice and arrange them attractively.

2   Place the vinegar, water, garlic, chilli, salt and spices into a pan and bring to the boil. Simmer for 5 minutes then pour over the courgettes, ensuring that they are completely covered by the vinegar. Seal. Will keep in the fridge for up to 2 weeks. Once opened, consume within 5 days.

FILLS 1 x 1-LITRE JAR

DROWNED TOMATOES

This is a lovely way to preserve all those tomatoes that you have lovingly grown (but perhaps just too many to eat) to use later in the year. Add them to pasta dishes, sauces and casseroles or to couscous salads.

INGREDIENTS

1 litre extra virgin olive oil
1 bulb of garlic, divided into cloves and lightly crushed
3 sprigs rosemary
2 sprigs thyme
1 sage leaf
salt and pepper
1kg small, cherry or plum tomatoes (a mix of yellow and red is nice)

METHOD

1   Gently heat the oil in a medium pan with the garlic and herbs for 5 minutes. Add the tomatoes, bring to the boil for 5 minutes then reduce the heat and cook for 15–20 minutes depending on their size, removing the smallest tomatoes first. As soon as the tomato skins split, remove the fruits with a slotted spoon so they do not overcook. You want the tomatoes to remain whole and just tender, not collapsing.

2   Remove the tomatoes with a slotted spoon and pack into a sterilised jar. Strain and pour the hot oil over the tomatoes ensuring they are completely covered. (If you have any oil left over, strain it and use it to make salad dressings and in cooking as it has a delicious flavour.) Seal with a lid and store for 1 week; once opened, keep in the fridge and use within 2 days.

MAKES 1 x 1-LITRE JAR

INDEX

Acknowledgements

Writing *The Patch* has been a delight and I'd like to thank the huge team that has both influenced it and helped to put it together.

Thanks to Emma Willis at the BBC and all at Silver River including Daisy Goodwin for her inspiration, Sam Chambers for her watchful eye, and Michael Kerr for his help as horticultural advisor and also his contribution to the photography. To Fern Britton for being so welcoming, and the three judges: Jim Buttress, Jonathan Moseley and Thane Prince for their extra input into the book, including Jonathan's special floral designs and Thane's pick of the best recipes from the programme.

Thanks to Nicky Ross from Hodder & Stoughton for her clear-visioned steering of the project and Sarah Hammond for her cool head against the deadlines, Jonathan Buckley for his breath-taking photographs, Mitzie Wilson for devising additional recipes and making up the recipes from the patch for photography, Helena Caldon for her swift and sensitive editing and keeping me on deadline target, Ashley Western for making the book look beautiful... and finally, Caroline Michel for having the vision to team me up with Daisy Goodwin at Silver River and Nicky Ross at Hodder & Stoughton.